AMERICAN SOCIETY:
What Poets See

Coeditors:
David Chorlton, Robert S. King

FUTURECYCLE PRESS

Mineral Bluff, Georgia

Published by FutureCycle Press
Mineral Bluff, Georgia, USA

ISBN 978-1-938853-08-1

FOREWORD

At the time this anthology reached the finishing stage, I had occasion to ride on the Texas Eagle Express. Starting out in the Texarkana station waiting room, I sat with a few other passengers watching a two-hour delay grow into three. They—some white, some black, all clearly less than affluent—looked accustomed to the service and took events in their stride. Once on board, I tried to forget about time and appreciate the journey as we passed small towns, forest, impressive houses proudly dominating their property, and shacks that appeared to be one gust of wind away from falling down.

Those of us who had boarded in Texarkana joined travelers who already had many miles behind them. One man complained that he had been on the train since Sunday, and this was a Thursday. Another, a likeable young fellow from New York with brightly tattooed arms, talked about girls, the New York streets, how it was fine to get a tattoo on your back but painful on the chest where there is little flesh, and endless movies. He talked about being laid off from his job as a car salesman because he hadn't sold a car in three days. Austin was his new place of promise, where jobs abounded and well drinks were cheap.

Through the windows of the observation car, Texas rolled by until our arrival in Dallas was announced. The young lady waiting at the door to get off said she rides the train often and expects it to be late. Some around us wore T-shirts advocating prayer or promising redemption. Others were wearing Batman shirts. Each of us in our way was having to deal with the way the Amtrak schedule falls short of its promises—just like the U.S.A. does —and although I was still torn between feeling annoyed at the delays and accepting them, we did finally arrive despite all the glitches on the way.

For this anthology, Robert and I have selected poems of the best quality from those submitted to us and have not solicited any submissions based on a personal basis or bias. Looking over the selections, I think about what we might have received but didn't. This anthology is not a representation of all sides of American society, and it doesn't contain a proportional number of poets from all backgrounds. Although I didn't expect any, I still find it interesting that we received no poems celebrating life in America from the point of view of a contented person: one happily married and still employed in this turbulent time, one with a nice house and garden. Either such people don't have the time or interest to write poetry, or they look outside of themselves when they do. Poetry as an art form, it seems, does not flourish through expressing complacency, so the project has turned out to be more like riding the Texas Eagle than a Cadillac. Personally, I'll go for the Eagle every time, in spite of the stops and starts. The spirit of poets here often strikes me as being a little bit like the fellow looking to start up in Austin, a place he can't have known well but one in which he will invest his energy to the utmost and hope for the best. We have contributors old (and wise) enough to tell us how life in America has changed over six decades and others who have gone up against the system in one way or another. This collective effort is not a testament to the vision of advertisers and business promoters; it is a record of what we poets see going wrong for our fellow travelers in a country that retains more than a little of Kinky Friedman's "Faded, jaded, falling cowboy star" to offset traditional optimism.

—David Chorlton

As David implies, few anthologies dealing with political and social themes offer a balanced viewpoint or broad enough coverage of the topic. American Society: What Poets See does not buck that trend. We asked for honesty, and indeed we got it from the many poets who submitted work to us. The contributors to this anthology come from all walks of life: blue collar, white collar, old and young, academic and lay.

In my experience, most poets are politically liberal-leaning, so it's no surprise that the themes of the poems reflect that position, even if the liberals occasionally do criticize their own side. What does surprise me is that we received only a few poems espousing an overtly conservative view. We would have liked to have included these voices but, unfortunately, the poems were not well enough written to publish. (If nothing else, this collection may confirm that the term "conservative poet" is an oxymoron.)

Our primary goal in assembling the anthology was to find as many good poems on as many relevant subjects as possible. There are still thematic gaps simply because we received no—or no worthy—poems on some topics. Not surprisingly, the poems make it clear that many poets are acutely aware of and concerned about the hard times that Americans are experiencing now. Many express frustration and despair, while others express hope in spite of the times. Some warn of what may happen if we do not change our ways; others say it is happening or has already happened.

I tend to be pessimistic about the future of America, but these poets comfort me even as they worry me because it's clear that I am not alone in my concern. It may sound like wishful thinking or arrogance, but I suggest we recognize that poets are the canaries in our coal mines: their songs carry meaningful trills that our society must listen to and act on. As a nation, we should understand that the sad and ugly things poets tell us come from hearts that long for fairness and compassion. Maybe such a notion is just spitting in the wind, but I like to think of these poets as our conscience.

—Robert S. King

POETS

POEMS BY THEME

Inequality and Injustice

Violence and War

AMERICAN SOCIETY:
What Poets See

AUSTIN ALEXIS

Accused

Sitting in prison for a crime
you didn't commit:
wrong multiplied to the tenth degree,
to the twentieth power.
First, you glow with indignation;
you drag it; it drags you.
You feel top-heavy with rage
so you topple over
into a region of disbelief
where nothing computes as real—
a fantasy land.
Your eyebrows freeze into question marks.
Then you steer your mind
toward a lucid zone,
commanding reason and facts
to drive you out of madness.

Later you reach for a rosary
as a person who's fallen overboard
flails for a life preserver
or as a drowning child
tries to grab a wave,
striving to make it stay still,
hoping to make it turn solid.

Finally you land on anger,
anger again.
You come ashore on its hot sand strip.
It's ablaze, and you are at home.
You're fired up with musings:
your sizzling past scorching the present.

The future stays bathed in harsh rays,
blinding you.
(Justice seems sightless in its own stupidity.)

Even shading your eyes
you can't penetrate beyond the glare
to stare into tomorrow.
And you can't get anyone else
to look in that direction, either.

GILBERT ALLEN

The Very Last Supper

*79% of recent college graduates do not support affirmative
action.... Their dream dinner guest is Jesus Christ.*
—Harris poll

They found Him
at Eternity Online, then downloaded
in His image from davinci.com.

He checked His Palm Pilate, said
sure, His stigmata were still open, but
could He bring a friend?

They only had service for twelve.

"He handles
his own silver."

That evening, in the vestibule, you could
pick them out right away, the only two robes
without data ports. For once, John
didn't say a word.

"Totally wireless," Tom whispered.
"Neural interface."

Turned out JC hadn't read
The Eleventh Commandment
or *Men Who Love Too Much.*
Judas shuffled away
from the buffet, when he found out
nobody named kids Judas anymore.

Matt got JC alone by the window, said
he was with the IHS, auditing
performance artists.
"You want *my* input? Lose

the hair, tattoo the thorns.
It's all deductible."

When they finally ran out of wine, Jimmy asked,
"Can you do a Merlot?"

Jesus shrugged. "This year OK?"

"You *can't* make a 27 C.E.?
Or you *won't*?"

He smoothed things over, lied
about the vintage, about the camels
and needles, let them know
He'd come to believe
in gated communities. Pete ashked
how He handled shecurity.

"Keyless. With retinal scans."

"Effing Alfa!"
"You the *man*!"

And Judas, surrounded
yet alone with his unspeakable
SATs, wondered why
his black ass'd been dragged
all the way down to hear
these future CEOs
blessing each other's brilliance—
until, leaning over that long table
of bodies and blood, he figured
this time he'd kiss them all.

Bees in Lavender

Only man's sick of blood,
and man's not so sick of it either.
—Robert Frost

Workaholics, hijackers
hover, bending every stalk
over in this city of stalks, un-
burdening each small window of nectar.

Only they can see through
to honey.

In a world for the moment
without birds, without breezes, without butterflies
they fill the mind
like the evening news
after a bad day.

Near the south end
of the newly mulched garden, their dance
turns to random music—something
between a radio reduced to static
and a dying electric razor.
I try to follow just

one—who fills its one
note with seventeen flowers
before I lose sight of it in the swarm
of likenesses. Lavender sways

toward sunset, becoming
the mirror that won't break, the windows
that keep falling.
On this feedback loop
in dying color, bees

become planes, become bodies
become planes, become bodies
until they all vanish at once.

Steady as vengeance,
flowers arise,
blue matches here and now
and now.

Maintenance Free Living

Admit it—it's what
we all long for, while we're waiting
for a prostate exam, or for the results
of an emergency lumpectomy, or
for an insurance agent's calendar
to finally clear.

All those eons ago, when Eden fell
and the lawnmower inevitably followed, we followed
behind it, dutifully—but we dreamed
of returning to an emerald world
perfectly maintained, without sod
webworms or army ants or the horrors
of chemical warfare. The Peaceable Kingdom

where every blade of grass
cut itself at precisely the proper
height and moment, every tulip
bloomed every glorious day, every juniper
swept up its own pollen.

So when I see those Technicolor promises
in the ever-growing advertising supplement
to my ever-shrinking daily newspaper

MAINTENANCE FREE LIVING

Hell yes, I'm more than tempted
by those yards about as big as a Pablo Kinkade
masterpiece, by those underground utilities, both electric and gas,
by those concrete driveways so short
somebody could shovel off their sugary snow with a teaspoon.

But that somebody, of course, wouldn't
be you. In your great room
you'd sit in front of your deserving

fireplace, fiddling with its remote control
like Itzhak Perlman, or Charlie Daniels,
depending on your weather of the day.

DIRECTV would select
your favorite programs—

If you have to ask, then what's the point?

would hang in needlepoint
above your microwave oven, which has just
sprouted legs, to bring you lasagna
to die for, and the perfect
funereal wine.

But do you really want Compassionate Conservatives
staring through their bathroom window
through your bathroom window
conservatively, ten feet away?
Do you really want Rover cowering
behind the commode, when you threaten
to take out his batteries?
Should Jesus, after all, be chained
to your Jacuzzi, eternally ready
to towel-dry your Methodist feet?

JENNIFER ARIN

Squash

Named in 1610 after the Lord
De La Warr, the state is home
to Dupont, once a gunpowder plant.
Mix 3 cups pumpkin, 3/4 cup honey
and a pinch of curry powder
for a killer pumpkin pudding.

Washington crossed its river
to war against 2 troops. Crush
1 pound pumpkin flesh, sauté
in butter, add white stock
for a soup of gold.

Slave-holders until the end
of 1865, punishing
women at the whipping post
till 1889, Delawareans were last
to abolish the pillory, 1905.
For No-Fault Squash,
mash 4 cups pumpkin
and 4 beaten eggs.

If you follow
the news, you might learn
that Delaware is home
to seventy thousand poor;
and that each Halloween,
its farmers use cranes
to hurl leftover pumpkins
far as a mile, over
their emptied patches.

Crowds cheer each smashed
squash. A reporter closes

his coat against the chill
and laughs, *What else could be
done with all those pumpkins?*

KATE BERNADETTE BENEDICT

After Long Days Visiting the Nursing Home, I Return to the Office

...to screen calls,
take minutes,
tweak numbers,
draft, deal, fax,
fix coffee,
smile the robotic smile.

How well everyone seems,
gesticulating forcefully,
walking unfalteringly on sound legs.
No one says *fork* when he means *briefcase,*
no one snores at the conference table
or slumps limply at her desk, dribbling.
Our chairs have wheels
but only so we can work faster,
swiveling deftly in the direction of vital purposes.

Odd, then, that breezing by a certain open door,
I catch sight of Manny, in his shirtsleeves,
motionless, emotionless, corpse-eyed,
no purpose in his eyes at all.
I hurry by
but sidewise I perceive his silhouette,
faint behind a scored glass wall.
His head is in his hands now,
his spine bows,
his weary posture an augury of times to come.

The Stinky Lady

Odd, how someone as small as our stinky lady
can stir up such large controversy.
Even in layers of old clothing, she is tiny,
altogether childlike in size,
though when asked to remove herself
from stoop or lobby,
she throws a child-size tantrum
and that's not small.
Aeaea! Aeaea! Aeaea!
They echo down the block,
the unnerving syllables of her fury.

She likes our building, its warm vestibule.
She rests inside on the couple of steps
behind our glass front door.
I pass her as I leave for work
and when I return from work.
Late at night, I watch her on closed-circuit television,
sitting quietly, as wide awake as I.
Does she sleep? Does she have a daughter?
Does she have a doctor, a PO box, a welfare check,
anything at all besides those threadbare clothes?

Somewhere, in some pocket or recess, she keeps makeup,
that rose lipstick she wears, the black eyeliner.
"I'm beautiful," I've heard her say,
peering into the cracked mirror of a compact.

"She's horrible," is the opinion of our co-op's board of directors.
They will add more locks
and fine any shareholder who lets her in.
Aeaea! Aeaea! Aeaea!
The feral call will echo not from this place,
but from a near place,

maybe every place.
The fact is, I see her everywhere I go:
on 57th Street, leaning
on Burberry's window in her dirty coat,
on Madison Avenue, crouching
on a curb in front of Gracious Home,
and on Broadway, dancing,
her made-up face uncanny in the neon glow.
Sooner or later,
policemen, doormen, proprietors
tell her to move on.
Aeaea! Aeaea! Aeaea!
Down the canyons of Manhattan
you can hear her wailing.
Aeaea! Aeaea! Aeaea!

Shrapnel

After Abu Ghraib

Not to complain, she says, but just to tell—
and keep it down kids, that's an awful clatter—
after suppers now she tweezes shrapnel
out of Vinny's back, a routine matter.

He's doing good, she says, his limp's improving.
He's drinking less and looking for some work.
If all goes well, soon they will be moving
off the army base and back home to West Burke.

The shards will just keep coming, though,
the smoother pellets and the jagged spikes.
She glides them from his body clean and slow.
He's quiet but she thinks that's what he likes.

She puts the pieces in a Mason jar
to stow among her staples and preserves,
an emblem right as any stripe or star.
She's doesn't pledge these days but she observes.

I wonder, cousin, if your Vinny's plight
mirrors in a way these times we're in.
Our nation's coping well enough, all right,
but are we being torn at from within?

Unceasingly, the souvenirs of terror—
fury, blind vindictiveness, and fright—
lead us into infamy and error.
One by one, the fragments come to light.

NINA BENNETT

I Don't Like Mondays

Sweet sixteen, she sprayed
a school playground with thirty rounds
from a semi-automatic 22 rifle,
a Christmas gift from her father.
She had asked for a radio.

Bullets pinged, popped,
ricocheted off a chain-link fence.
Third graders huddled in the weeds.
Principal, midway through his first year,
dead. His wife saw the news
flash across her TV screen. Custodian
killed as he ran to help. Twenty-eight
year old cop, badge still shiny,
injured, eight kids shot.

Barricaded inside her house
for seven hours before she surrendered,
no remorse, she told police
I don't like Mondays, this livens up the day.

I dread Monday mornings, have to force myself
out from under the covers when the alarm blares.
I could never go on a shooting spree. At least,
I don't think I could. Pregnant
with my second son, my palm rests
on the firm swell of my abdomen.

The Laramie Project

I take my grandson to a fall festival
where he makes a scarecrow
by stuffing discarded jeans
and a plaid flannel shirt
with straw. He digs
through the pile of clothes
until he finds a shirt
the same color as his.
He wrestles and pummels
the arms and legs
with ferocious determination;
the violence of his young hands pounding
the scarecrow into shape disturbs me.
We bring his creation home,
tie it to a section of fence
along my garden. Its shoulders and hips
droop where there isn't enough straw;
images of Matthew Shephard,
beaten and tied to a snow fence
on the desolate plains outside Laramie,
distort my vision. After my grandson
returns home I untie his scarecrow
and lay it to rest on the shed floor,
cover it with the blanket
we use for picnics. Certainly
any parent would wish this respect
for his child. Tomorrow
I will explain to my grandson
my rescue of his scarecrow,
and hope this will lessen
my lingering guilt
that at the time of Matthew's death
I didn't say enough.

KEVIN BROWN

There Are Rules

It is just a grocery store, but there are rules:
the bagger must bag

all beer unless he (or she) is under
eighteen, at which point the customer or cashier
must cover it; stickers from fresh
fruit are not allowed

on nametags, as they cover the corporate
logo; similarly, nicknames are forbidden, as are attempts
to be clever, with names such as Clyde
or Elvis, as impersonating

others could cause customer complaints
to be misfiled, even though it is just
a grocery store; there are rules:
buggies

are called bascarts, baggers, courtesy clerks,
who must put ten items in each bag by building
the sides first then fill
the middle, plastic, the default, unless the patron pushes
for paper, cloth bags a nuisance

to be tolerated, as the customer is convinced
they will save the planet, even though it is just
a grocery store; there are rules:
all employees must be back
from break in under fifteen minutes
unless a shift exceeds six hours, though only a few

full-time employees, mainly minor
managers, make enough to earn
such shifts, while Ryan returns to his register,

back from the hospital, no health
benefits to supplement his surgery
expenses after his not-technically-full-time five years
here because, after all, it is just
a grocery store, and there are rules.

MELISSA CARL

"Want to Know Who We Are?"

Forget the quiet poem about pine trees,
the poem where the speaker goes into the woods
and feels kind of religious.

Gulp down the poems that burn,
poems of land mines and sudden dark,
of blindfolds and courtyard executions---

poems that sit in the mud
of refugee camps
and eat mice in the tents.

Hear the strange sobs of poems
under the surreality of TV news
where two minutes of blood and tanks

precede two minutes of breakfast cereal.
Don't believe them when they tell you
how pleasant the weather was today.

Return to the barbed wire poems,
the moments of bomb smearing children
into the gutters while only the smoke escapes.

Forget Dante and his Circles
where cause and effect
explain the suffering.

Want to know who we are?
Read the poem in which the river rises
towards the village the entire night

and the moon refuses to watch.

DAVID CHORLTON

Cheap Mangos

There's an easy flow of music through
the speakers at the supermercado
where papayas ripen while you watch
their skins disintegrate
the way a man's skin does
when he's found on his back in the desert
facing the sun with his mouth locked
between a scream and a prayer. His trouser leg
is torn where a coyote
came to gnaw at his thigh
and of his right forearm only
the bones remain, while on his left wrist
a watch still measures time.
The music has a teardrop in its beat
and nostalgia in the singer's voice
but the juice aisle is a happy place
with any flavor you'd remember
from a trip across the border
going south to a colorful village
with peppers stacked in the market
just like these red, green, yellow ones
displayed in the order of their bite,
a village likely similar
to one the woman left
whose sweater clings to what remains
of her where she collapsed
in a pair of sports shoes good for many
more miles with the tread on their soles
and Just Do It style. Something pulled at her hair
where her scalp peeled away
but the strap on her brassiere
is indestructible as the belt
that falls slack where the flesh has wasted
from her hips. Had she made it

to a road she might have found
her way to Phoenix, to the store
where the cakes in the cold case
are churrigueresque, and mangos
are two for ninety-nine cents.

Economics

—A sudden shower
of light
falls on the man
whose flask is dry

and he surrenders again.
A dozen times
he has made a run;
each time
with more water,

but it is never enough.
He cannot carry
a river. Still,
he comes back

over and again:
walking on stones,
in the hold of a ship,
sleeping upright
in a cattle car,
dying en route,

then taking work
the living have already refused.

Coming Summer

The geckos come out from cracks
in the house walls where
warmth soaked through their skins in winter
and cling like condensation
to the ceiling of the porch,
pale in the white light the lamp
by the door spills across them.
They are the portent of a summer

through which the lost will wander
and evaporate inside their clothes;
when the print on maps will fade in the sun
before anyone can read directions;
when the round Earth will give way
to a flat one that tilts
into hallucination. What is distant
will appear as close at hand

from the break in the horizon
where smugglers carry their backpacks
to the end of a road
whose white lines curl back
to tie a knot for the union
of poverty and risk. Those with money
will place it in cold storage

while those without
will be armed and ready but have
no one to turn on
but themselves. They will be shown
on late night television
between the game show and the infomercial

selling instructions for success
at a price rising with the temperature.

To the Man on Death Row, Waiting

It's a fine day
with the air being clear after recent rain
and a coolness now the long
summer has ended. I'm looking at a picture
of the room prepared
for your final breath, with its bar of artificial light
above a kind of bed set
with sheets as if it were in a hospital
you would be in to be healed, and the long
dark window on the other side
of which the seats are empty now.
The walls could be beige, almost
a color, as if blue or green
would have been more than you deserved.
It's after three, the trees outside here
are filled with birdsong and in the distance
is the long, repeated note
of the whistle on a freight train gathering speed
for the miles of desert
it will cross before nightfall.
Nobody knows yet
whether this is your final day, with all
the appeals and last minute attempts
to keep you alive, but whether or not
tomorrow happens I hope
you enjoyed the fried okra, steak well done,
ice cream and Dr. Pepper drink. I'm listening
to the radio for news amid that of the killing
in war that goes on every day
for word that one death
will be avoided. Looking out
at the winter lawns beginning to sprout along
our street, and the shadows
lengthening across them, it is hard
to imagine the world reduced to a room, and time

to a countdown. Clear skies tonight, the forecast says,
and fine tomorrow, when the train
will be crossing Texas with a rumble like a thousand
hearts determined never to stop.

ALEX CIGALE

Habeas Corpus (Show Me the Body)

In America, we do not torture.
We slap your face drooping, eyes glazed over,
deprived of sleep, dripping with splashed water
from a glass smashed when you beg for a drink,
left standing naked and exposed to the cold,
as in the beginning, as we all were of old.

You've got to listen and do as you're told
hands manacled hanging from the ceiling,
on cement floor shivering without a blanket,
in pretrial detention denied human contact
enemy of the state, enemy combatant.
Certain well-established, proven effective

psychop methods like sexual shaming
and having you piss and shit on yourself
are perfectly suitable and appropriate
to root out those evil doers, the terrorists.
The prisoner's dilemma: we only want
to know; please tell us what we want to hear.

JAMES CIHLAR

Ideology Begins at Home

*March 23, 2010, President Obama signs
health care reform into law*

If my father believed in time cards,
in sleeping on the sofa in his work clothes
on Sunday mornings, my mother believed in privacy,
in attending a different church every week,
where no one would recognize us,
so we could take communion
without going to confession.

My mother believed in brunch at Bishop's Buffet,
Petula Clark, Tom Jones, *Cosmopolitan,*
figural perfume bottles, rearranging the furniture,
coordinating separates.

My father believed in Porter Wagoner, Conway Twitty,
Johnny Cash, making his own furniture,
Mad Magazine, the draft,
having something to fall back on,
returning to his parents' farm
after the divorce, telling me
to get a teaching certificate in college.

Both were indifferent to LBJ and Spiro Agnew.
They both believed in Original Sin,
in throwing salt over your shoulder,
in crossing your fingers, in not crying
over spilled milk, in looking beautiful,
in the New Deal,
and the Great
Society.

I believe in *The Big Lebowski, Family Guy,* pore strips,
the sentient power of animals,

sleeping late,
and disco
as the exhilarating soundtrack
for the last
generation
who believed,
like today's,
anything
is possible.

JIM CLARK

One Late Night

I heard Phil Ochs on internet radio
One night late as I worked from my home
In an outlying province of the old imperial
Lost and forsaken U. S. of A.

And Richard Fariña was harmonizing sweetly
To a song that I knew but had never heard
In the pre-dawn light of the millennial morning
I scratched these words on the back of a bill

Chorus:

Loaves and fishes and horses and wishes
The virgins go begging to the cold-hearted bridegroom
If Jesus was here he'd climb back on the cross
He'd walk straight back in the shadows of the tomb

Now it's thirty springs since the chair and the belt
And forty dark years on a fast motorbike
The country you loved is a dream you took with you
Now it's monkeys and demons and the ghost of John Train

Where men of the cloth preach murder and hate
And leaders are liars who prove war is peace
One nation under a vengeful God
Whose son disappeared on the road to right now

Chorus

A mourning dove sang from a bush by my window
As a squad of Blackhawks roared up from the south
They're practicing up for their appointment in Samarra
Then all was quiet, the bird it had flown

Chorus

KELLY CLAYTON

Justine Takes Off

Thirty minutes on stage, thirty working the barstools,
I change into vintage corset and easy
to remove evening gown, the other girls put on make-up, razor bikini
lines, count dollars falling from glittery drawstring purses.

I slide onto a stool next to dry mouthed pez dispenser,
and ask if he wants to talk
for a price.
No resting Pleezer platforms without
a sweaty drink in hand.

Shirley Temple every fifteen minutes means
I'll have to pee during my next set, make it even harder to get off
the stage for hand-to-hand tips.

Mr. Dispenser's time is up,
I roll onto the stage, carbonated belly sloshing.
Desiree beat me to the good spot, she stares at Coke Bottle Glasses sitting
at three o'clock. She smells like peaches.

Annie Lennox asks important questions through busted speakers,
while above my head the Knicks also lose
their shirts.

My bag lies on its side, tied to upstage pole
behind Lula Boy, pulling draft beers for the post office.
I reach behind, and touch railroad tracks in silver lamé
my dress opens, a split catfish nailed to a cypress.

I take bills held like cigarettes between two fingers,
and know that the answer is yes,
I would lie to you.

CHELLA COURINGTON

Insomnia

You recognize me   strolling streets   to be with people   without
being   with people   You ask for one dollar   One dollar

What if I only have a twenty   Can I owe you   tonight
your eyes   bloodshot like mine   bags   holding them   back

Samuel Johnson   roamed   London   midnight   to sunrise
Couldn't bear   the garret   stacked   in words   amanuenses oblivious

to stale air   his rambling Fleet   my rambling State   slipping   in my skin
bleak above   cement days   disintegrating   unseen   except by you

grave lady   reaching   for me   singing a hymn   Johnson sang   Binding
he squeezed   for more   than God   could give   Dust   in his palm

When nothing else would help   love   *lifted*   *me*   I'm not him   can't
take you home   I offer this bill   & all the change   in my pocket

BARBARA CROOKER

Summary, 2010

Dear future generations: Please accept our apologies.
We were rolling drunk on petroleum.
—Kurt Vonnegut

The wine-dark sea was slick with oil.
Pelicans struggled in the viscous surf,
foamy waves clotted with tar balls,
an obscene green sheen.
Sea turtles lumbered ashore,
dragged darkness behind them.

Politicians kept spewing rhetoric
and lies. BP stations beckoned
with their sunflower logos,
but we knew better, saw
that the words of their CEO
didn't match his eyes....

The sun set each night
like a smear of mustard.
Earth's black arteries
opened, and the pressed

blood of dinosaurs
flowed and flowed....

And we kept the lights on;
we kept on driving our overly

large cars. The shrill
sound of drilling replaced
the cicadas, became
our new national anthem....

Catalog

It's February, and we're freezing, despite global climate change,
despite the melting ice caps. It seems that winter comes later now,
that the seasons are askew. But here in the pages of my L. L. Bean
Catalog, a fire is blazing brightly, *natural resin fatwood sticks*
bringing it to life, and a *mallard blue hearth rug* protects my floors.
Warmth is guaranteed no matter what the winter brings: a blizzard
of bad news from the television, the icy rain of losses—age chipping
away at the body, a flurry of Christmas cards where sorrow
tipped the scale away from joy. The radio hisses
its static: another car bomb explodes in Iraq like the rat-

tat-tat of sleet; predictable as a cold front marching
down from Canada. But in these glossy pages, we are told
that *when you select your outerwear, you should consider*
your personal response to cold, your activity levels,
local weather conditions. Locally, I'd say the weather
is conservative, with a touch of paranoia. Our ears,
whether covered by a *Mountain Guide Hat in Moss Khaki*
or a *Stone Blue Fleece Headband,* seem closed to the larger
world, deaf to the voices of want and need. We give
what we can, but not so much it hurts. Somewhere in the city,
a man sleeps in a cardboard box. A woman and a child huddle
under a blanket on a subway grate. We pass by quickly,
wrapped in goosedown and Gore-Tex. The wind keeps
on blowing, as it always will.

J. P. DANCING BEAR

David in the Glass City

   I am not the boy
with the sling shot.
And Goliath is not a sky scraper.
With every pane, I can see something
I was or will be—
as watery as the past remains.
Someone wears a sandwich
board that notes, *Jesus Loves You*
—a moment's comfort, I'm sure—
but I know he's seeing
other people.
Like glass and cloud and steel,
polished to perfection—
the universe in reverse—
not the evil and its twin, not
shadow boxing, not *never talk*
about fight club, not yin, not yang—
but belief. Not only an imagined
self but the world around the self:
silvered and better than this one—
heaven? Jesus surfing the cumulus
   and all the souls
locked away in their glass cages.
I never had to believe in the rock
or the slingshot—I just know
they make fast work of mirrors.

Election Season

The old politicians are on their way
to the tall ashes of the state, beyond all hope
of green and lighted fields before the hills.

In a different place, the dead might drift
down the river as campaigners move
into the weeds of the pale city, set up camps,
alive with promises of work. But it is Autumn
and the geese have already begun to feel
the fading light within their wings.

The volunteers can hardly feel the cold
as they pin another button on the coat
of a slender farm child. The gray light does
not fill these skies with hope;
neither can the pumpkins manifesting
themselves in the twilight;
nor the ghosts of river boats
paddling slowly against the current.

The candidates flow into the city with the moon
upon the withering fields white with frost.
All are reflecting a brightness
that is not theirs to keep or give.

ERICA DAWSON

A Poem That's Not a Song or Set in the South

Maryland, my Maryland, a border line,
"Free State," disordered North/South, mountain pine
Cones west, bald cypress at the Bay, with brine

Along the coast and snow in Hagerstown,
White Oak, blue crab, orange and black, and down
The Ocean, *hon,* that January brown—

Do we even have a song? A soothing sound
Of the south? I want the taste, touch, wet mouth round
About the vowels in every guitar drowned-

Out syllable. My cousins have a twang.
I have a Mid-Atlantic pitch. Notes hang
Near a middle C. I say, *I'll do my thang?*

That just won't work. O, say, but can I see,
Say, quirks ("lacks natural lakes"), state oddity,
(One part's a mile wide) and sights (D.C.,

Where Lincoln's waiting)? In another place,
At the Potomac, dancing on my face,
A zephyr, boa-like, but commonplace

As my perfume, nuzzles against my chin.
Our Maryland version of a Chinook comes in,
Descending off the Rockies' next-of-kin

In Appalachia. Sing to me now; and, wrap
Up all my naked skin. I want to nap
In its nook, wear its dress, and scotch its stocking cap,

Then follow it along to Arlington,
Another other place. There, I'd lie in sin
On soldiers marked unknown. The air is thin

And thick as if it offers up a cure,
A viscous antidote and I am sure
Of this "America in Miniature,"

And anecdotes so much I know the pinned
And bowing Black-eyed Susans almost grinned,
Black-faced, enough to keep my peeled eyes skinned.

DIANE ELAYNE DEES

Lament for Louisiana

Each day the fragile coastline slips away,
a sedge, a heron's home, an eagle's nest,
will vanish before the sky folds into gray.

The egrets in the Atchafalaya Bay,
the marsh hen with its shining azure crest—
each day the fragile coastline slips away,

leaving no safe place for them to stay.
The spoonbill with the banded golden breast
will vanish. Before the sky folds into gray,

you still can see a glorious display,
as the roseate sun glides slowly to the west
each day. The fragile coastline slips away

as bold raccoons and river otters play.
The black bear, who was once a welcome guest,
will vanish before the sky folds into gray.

The rich blue view of iris in array
alongside swamp rose mallow finely dressed—
each day the fragile coastline slips away—
will vanish before the sky folds into gray.

ANTHONY DIMATTEO

County Fair, Memorial Day

Ski hats pulled on tight, high
heels and shorts, obese men
wearing skeletons as decor, rings
in noses, tongues, and ears, tattoos
of dragons, baby's feet, dropping bombs,
the face of Jesus turning an arm
into Veronica's veil—and that's just the line
queuing up for the Zipper ride. Come
and see the show. Which one? Across the way,
Alice, a magician's large white rabbit,
pees on a little boy offered up
by his parents. Children and animals
are sure to make us reach. Wolves—
WILD WOLVES the sign insists—pace
back and forth as the smell
of sausage fills the air. Do we look
like pigs to them while we text
madly waiting for the horror house?
(Nimble hooves work tiny keys.) I look up
into the eyes of the alpha male, golden brown
the better to see at night, the hawker tells me,
but who needs to see inside a cage?
Now the wolves look lost amidst
a gawking crowd. I recall
the primal terror that ran up my spine
alone in Yellowstone deep in the woods
when off in the distance as sun set
I heard the pack howl. Out of the wild,
invisible walls close in. One's coerced
to walk the line the world assigns
as thine and mine split us in two.
Borders and borders and borders have us
pace back and forth. We duck our heads
when a three-gun salute to the troops goes off.
When I played with toy soldiers,

I was always the safe general far away.
Another fantasy was to join a circus
traveling up and down the east coast
or the big highways out west, living
in a community of fellow free ones,
bit of straw in our mouths as we sit
exhausted after hauling out tents.
Trying to rescue my lost dream,
I shuffle through the crowd
to speak to a woman working a stand.
Lou Ann, her nameplate says, looks at me
with tired eyes. She laughs. "The job's
got its moments, but the magic's gone.
The work is hard and there's barely any relief."
Later I see her walk by through the mass
of us, making her way to the trailer park
new sprung in some parking lot seen
by outsiders only from the Ferris wheel:
potted plants and satellite dishes,
a few residents mulling about smoking
as the night drops down on all of us.

Work

On one side of the wall, men
grade the street yet again.
On the other side, I grade
papers, A, B, C or F.

They stop to talk of wives,
then shovel and broom the tar.
I've paused to listen,
struck by the light.

To flatten out a line,
a pen will do.
Who needs a steamroller?
A frog's-view takes a poem.

To see oneself seeing oneself
before road or word
gets graded, that's steep
on both sides of the wall.

In view of this work, we
are the same. The other side
of the path remains wild
and rolls endlessly towards us.

DAVID EBENBACH

Looking for a Job

What you want, at least, is the dignity
of a Sisyphus—you want to see yourself
on a hilltop, your muscles and hands
afire and chest roaring for breath, and
that boulder and its pounding descent
seen at least through your memories
of the throne. But the elevator hauls
you to another unstoried floor, another
hard carpet trod by the many, and your
one suit has a stain at the shoulder, and
you carry your account along the hallway
with the growing sense that it weighs
nothing at all. What weighs, really, is
the fear that this is your myth, this drag
up the hill with empty, tender hands,
and the ride back down again—untold
by gods or men how, during the slow
fall, you take off your suit jacket and
pick at the stain until it becomes a hole.

Friday Afternoon in Brooklyn

The siren spreads across Brooklyn and I, so long
in the Midwest, first think it's a severe weather

warning, like the night we found a neighbor's
basement while a tornado moved past

Richmond, Indiana, and we were possessed
by elaborate imaginings of a twister along 4th Street,

but in Brooklyn the siren just means
Shabbat, a warning about

Shabbat. They say it's 100 decibels, same as
a motorcycle or a snowmobile. In Brooklyn

Shabbat is serious, comes at you like summer weather.
Judaism is serious in Brooklyn—when the young

women pedal by in hipster t-shirts, in skirts past
Satmar eyes, the city has to paint over the bike lanes.

And the hipsters have to repaint them
under their videocameras at night. In Brooklyn

youth is serious, and so is the blog. In southwest Ohio
Christianity is serious, the churches with their

signs out front, *No Freedom But In Christ,* or
Don't Make Demands Of God—Await His

Instructions. Even the funny ones—*To Avoid Burning,*
Apply Son-Screen—even the Touchdown Jesus statue

struck by lightning, not so funny. Once on the ride
between these places, we see a sign—*Your*

Parents Are Lying to You About Santa—and
a phone number to call. Alongside all this, another farm.

Farms everywhere, advertising McDonald's, milk,
God in various forms. We drive the landscape

at illegal speeds, serious about getting through.
For those two days, the car is our place, like

the invented under-the-bed country of a child.
Radio static, road noise; Ohio becomes Pennsylvania

becomes New York, where old traffic thunders and we
step stunned into another space. Foldout couch,

guest room, childhood bed reclaimed. Windows
over Brooklyn, the people walking, the BQE,

the delivery trucks. All the urgent tasks of the day.
In Ohio the freight trains howl over the towns and

fields every morning. Now, in the air—it's all
summer out there, all sun, no sign of storm

or the end of the day—the siren stops after
maybe a minute. People take off their aprons,

bring down their stores' metal shutters or
don't. Clean their stations for closing or

don't. They've heard the siren. They head home
if they're going to, or turn their eyes

back to their work. In any case they step
toward something. Everyone has decided

what to do next; everyone knows what's coming.

ALAN ELYSHEVITZ

The Card

is required for transport to all points beyond
a radius. It is speckled with biometric data:
inseam, girth, dosage of melanin. How many
flecks of green in predominantly blue eyes.
The tips of the cardholder's fingers, those divine
snowflakes. Follicles losing integrity, at what rate.
Voice print: the cardholder's peculiar dialect,
the sloppy vowels of local geography. The card
measures REM, when the cardholder falls
asleep at the wheel, and records all DUI's,
as well as the cardholder's chronic passions
for minor league baseball and Byzantine art.
The card is the cardholder's anti-ephemeral
manifesto. Though nearly two dimensional,
it embraces generations of dispirited ancestors
and temporarily innocent offspring. In this way
its lamination is as deep as a pool of DNA.
If the card has a soul, it has absorbed it from you.

MARGOT FARRINGTON

Foreclosure

That wasn't the place we bought, but think
how long it's mortgaged memory. That
seller striving mightily to please.
Dining room, he said, but we could alter
that. Second bedroom—perhaps we'd want
to make it work space? Tidy, I recall. House
situated in a hollow. The claim of the '49 Chalmers tractor
and the dog's unusual name.

Immaculate barn. We'd have cut the
umbilicus three generations long:
been first not to farm this place. Those
bales destined for mulch or nothing at all, the pile
hauled out: ziggurat sinking into muck.
Would clean Holsteins help to sell? His were
buffed dominos, watching from their stanchions.

Jubal. That was the dog's name.
Again, he hits the end of his chain. I hear the
choke closing on windpipe, squeezing frenzy to a
whisper. His dance nearly a gallows waltz, and
his prayer a wolf's prayer.
Lines from an old song come unbidden;
they're troubling me today:

See there those strangers comin'
See them there, those you don't know
See there the strangers comin'
lookin' quick and talkin' low
You don't live here anymore
you soon will have to go...

RUPERT FIKE

Watering in a Drought

—after Knoxville Summer, 1915

In his four-page paean to a gone time
James Agee as a boy watched fathers
watering their twilight lawns with
   ...a tenderness of spray that produced
   a quiet deep joy, too real to recognize itself...

But tonight I am denied such joy
for I have come to know too much—
the information age as a burden.
I know the reservoir's down for one thing,
the crimes of this century past another.
Planet's on the ropes with a split lip,
swollen as these stress-cracked tomatoes,
my ugly babies. And here's Aquarius
bearing water on the odd-number day.
Or are all days now odd, beyond sad pales?
Still I spray, but it's not a bit tender
because I'm using my thumb, drips forming
to trickles down the hose, wetting my shoes,
not at all what I wanted. Precious waste.

Agee and his joy in a midtown taxi,
dead, keeled over from a burst heart
yet spared seeing World Without End
exposed as finite same as its mortals,
his generation the last lucky bunch
to bask in the potbellied warmth of faith
in all fathers, when humankind was good,
incapable of deeds we now know we've done.
And so I water while wishing I wasn't
or wishing I was little-boy Agee
back when each opened spigot was comfort,
back when all hoses fed from God's lake.

ALISSA FLECK

Mitchellville Penitentiary Maximum Security Prison for Women

I am the offspring of a keychain adultery,
a Thanksgiving-ruiner, a threat
to society—

a spiral-bound shank wielder, a moonshine
brewer, a lock your trunk
or she'll climb in-er.

My ponytail climbs like a carnival ride.

I'm not like anybody here but I talk like it
because that's what you do.
I make love to other women behind washing machines
because that's what you do too

and when I write about it, I write about war;
I write about wars and the way they sound and
washing machines.

I pray for tampons and not
salvation. Yes,

I stabbed him twenty-six times. Yes,

I took his credit cards and I went shopping.

BARBARA GABRIEL

Closer to God and Sin

When I look back on Bud I know
the scrape of sharp whiskers on a child's unripened cheek.

The tarry taste of Chesterfields
in a goodbye kiss, until he ceased smoking
seventy years after he had begun,
when a carton went to twenty bucks and that was too damn much.

I know the crack of bat on ball, rumble of a crowd
and the announcer, rapturous, over radio waves
being the one genuine way to follow baseball.

That smoky Saturday nights spent at the St. Paul Auditorium
were better than church,
don't let that Loretta next door tell you otherwise,
because All-Star wrestling got you closer to God and sin.

I know that Bud married a Rebel woman
one month to the day after she hollered *G'wan Yankee, get off my porch*
and revered her for the rest of his days.

That being the fastest swimmer was no proof
against his baby brother disappearing under the sullen, silent surface.

Calloused, meaty hands tough enough for chopping cotton
also held a brass-and-mahogany level straight and true,
creating beauty from board.

That love grew in impenetrable places
if you recognized that you were brave and let your own light shine.

I know that an old man and a six-year-old girl
could break the world's record for time and speed
on a run from Marshall, Texas to Minnesota,
with a Folger's can and a sharp lookout
and Buck Owens on the 8-track.

Invisible

Everyone knows
about the dreaded knock,
an officer in blues

and a chaplain.
But few have heard
about erasures.

We see the gleam
of silver trumpets, hear
"Taps" and volleys from

seven soldiers firing,
feel fabric of a flag
folded and pressed

into hands of a woman
dressed in black.
From this moment on

she is invisible, cast out
from base housing
before neighbors

sense shadows
creeping across
their own lawns.

Moving vans steal away
in middle of night.
Everyone greets the new

family with smiles,
pies filled with apples
and relief.

LES GOTTESMAN

Megatrends

Gestures complete the platitude
we dance with death for death's oil.

Yes, there is a voice that turns cartilage to soup
last seen walking a huge dog over the locked earth

and yes, ever since the cyborg generation
whose fulfillment in demise in San Francisco I watched

the sky glows like the town's on fire in the rain.
A tree leans downhill on the slopey street, chewing vapor,

and woodenly responsive to the crisis of its time,
which is long, retains its useless freedom.

Trilobite

We like a sturdily built man with short curly hair
casually but appropriately dressed
calm in demeanor
but aggressive in action.
In him we breathe
the last interviews with our children.

Captives Backlit

Lay down your choices of world,
lay down. The long and last slaughter begins
in the heart of Texas. Very Alamo. Lay down.

Oil is the dangling mouth that ripped the head off Mabel.
The reich is best regulated with detonated sleep.
Many massaged feet thank you for what you are doing
that you don't know about yet.

Oil or women, whatever it is you have sent
will not be returned to you
but will pay forward the advances in paw and claw
that drag you burning behind.
Let those who cannot understand misunderstand.

MICHAEL GREGORY

Pins and Needles

> *recessions were induced*
> —William Greider

Who will tell the people
the secrets of the temple?

madness in high places
high crimes *contra natura*

the coin of the realm minted
in nomine populi

then taken away as taxes
from those who have least

given as *droit de seigneur*
to private interests

returns on savings so low
everyone buys on time instead

mortgages on homes foreclosed
homeless and jobless in the streets

then borrowed back in a lender's market
ungodly profits on treasury notes

the major banks bailed out
while farms go broke and factories close

the dealers in arms and currency
never at a loss in a pinch

compounding the national debt
with personal bankruptcies

borrowing at interest
the practical fiction of legal tender

the sins of the fathers and so forth
genius vilified or ignored

to pay for all the common wealth
squandered on such insanities—

war, corruption, pollution, PR—
forked tongue on forked tail

the high priest of the state religion
the chief talking head of the bank of issue

intoning monetary dogma
blessing the puppet in the oval office

whose fiscal policy belies the myth
of representative democracy

determining between them how flat
the little guy will get squeezed

in the interest of high interest
how fat the bubbles will be inflated

how thick the cloud of speculation will be
spread by those who buy and sell debt

how high the unemployment will rise
before the point of the pin trade is factored in

LOIS MARIE HARROD

Bread

Sometimes the past returns,
as a student whose knees
seemed too narrow to bear

his classmates' jeers,
queer, faggot,
his voice so foreign

you astonish yourself
when you call out his name,
Michael and it is.

he's traded his thin white arms
for a leather jacket and shoulders
broad enough to hang a sleeve,

a soldier now, holding
the sky above Somalia
an ebony bowl in his hands.

His friends have told him
to write the stench of Mogadishu,
he has friends now,

but he wants to tell you
about the white stars rising above the desert,
and as he looks at your ceiling,

the lights seem to float
like a basket of bread in the evening.
Thus he begins singing his songs,

this boy whom you do not remember
saying a word in your class, his voice
now a white loaf in the sand

and all around, the students
roll up their eyes from their dry study
as if they too were hungry

and you wonder what crust
you could have thrown him
that made him come back to you today.

Dumb Fuck

dying in friendly fire

You are someone's tragic supper, love apple moaning
as the fridge slams shut, six months gone and the June wedding trips
down the stairs, who will deliver it now, that child of yours, moths flit
the only streetlight on your street, the one you used to jiggle

to watch go out like a breath.

How were they to know you were in front of them,
your father, your brother, the mother who got away,
the pregnant one you emailed nearly every day? How did you get *there*
when you left them *here* choking down their beef?

Look at the gewgaws spread on your bed, the stuffed teddy,
the football, your velvet thighs gone in a quake of sundown sparrows.
They spell your short story, *cheap cheep,*
how light burst your downy belly, oh Achilles, how slippery

you were on the way out, thought you would always...be.

Now the quiet time, the past with the baby still
howling in the blanket. Didn't that mother of yours wrap you in orange
to carry you from the car, afraid of deer hunters in the woods?
Weren't there trumpet vines beneath your bedroom window

warning the hummingbirds? Wasn't there an umpire crying OUT
to the boy breaking his own leg with his own bat?
Why didn't someone tell you,
don't wear red, white or blue during a turkey shoot.

MICHELLE HARTMAN

Reality TV

we hurried
through dinner
left dishes soaking
pre-execution show
six central
sure to be good
hostile—violent
repeat offender
killed entire
family in their
sleep

crime scenes
on highlights

sure enough
he kicked
screamed
all the way
to the table

great last speech
hate filled
with threats
claims—of innocence
fought the straps
until final seizure

recent ones were
    quiet
        calm
critics charged
drugging
this should
boost ratings

quick bathroom break
eight o'clock
large strafing
planned in Jalalabad
body count high

and falling, fly

I

according to Zen philosophy
we are to leap and the net
will appear
while this may work for old
monks it does not occur to well-bred Southern
girls who carry matches in their purses
to mask their odors in public restrooms
never eat food from homes they
have not visited
gentle Southern women who never return
an empty dish and know how to insult with sublime
grace, too polite to ask what anyone earns
yet always knows what everyone is worth

but good Southern women have begun to drown
their children, burn their husbands in sunshine
fragranced sheets and vote for black men

II

I repeatedly watch
City of Angels, the scene
where the angel puts his arms out
and tips forward into nothingness
to become human, to feel

and I want to fly—not caring
if the net appears—
I'll smoke dark brown cigarettes, drink
straight whiskey, talk to strangers
and wake hard
next to a nameless man bearing circus-
sized genitalia, in between times we'll burn
my Daughters of the Confederacy
membership card

M. AYODELE HEATH

The Dreamlife of Dr. Bledsoe's Inner Pickaninny

> *Bledsoe, you're a shameless chitterling eater! Ha! And not only*
> *do you eat them, you sneak and eat them in private when you*
> *think you're not being observed! ...I accuse you of indulging*
> *in a filthy habit, Bledsoe! Lug them out so we can see!*
> *I accuse you before the eyes of the world!*
> —Invisible Man *from Ralph Ellison's* Invisible Man

Though he long ago resumed consuming pork,
to this day he still will not eat fried chicken
in front of White folk (Octoroons,
or even Negroes he needs
to impress). Pondering entrées
at a recent business lunch, craving the crunchy,
peppered crust, his glands moisten
   at the mere thought.
                              But he fears
the Black skillet's neon grease will wildly distort
the innate thickness of his lips. That sucking a drum-
stick dry will expose the enormous
ivory bone stuck through his nose, warping
his face, weighing him down in an apelike walk
till his meticulous pin-striped life unravels
   like an unruly raffia skirt.

Thus, when dessert time comes, he avoids sweet
potato confections, pecan confrontations, and other
denigrating delectables at all costs. Instead,
his controlled fork picks (like a good little
boy) through cool fruit salad. Devouring apples,
cherries, pears and grapes, he leaves a clean White
plate—curiously bare but for
   watermelon parts.

Asked why he will not eat them, his reply:
Where would I hide
   the seeds?

KATHLEEN HELLEN

Belly Song

I sit in the front row of
bleachers—cheap seats for greater grief.
My son

the tribe in his ribs
the strength in him, keen, huddled
runs through the hits, breathes
through the pale ghost of stitches
these games that go long into hard victories.

Who knows how long we have them?
when sirens call to the streets
when one sends back his fatigue

another's enlisted.

The bones of an open Humvee. The bones
at a roadside checkpoint.

It might be that we swallow them:
A belly song. A flag sent home.
A rosary like dog tags.

A triage of crows flies over.
My son

packs up his cleats.
The fog of his breathing surrenders.
He limps to the car where I tender
his wounds. The bones
of a cradle, breaking.

A Congress of Monsters

A long grey chin reminds you
of Sacco and Vanzetti at a funeral.
You're cynical. Too thin
to costume doubt. Too transparent
in the mask that sometimes answers
squad cars on the block. Sometimes knocks
Devils in the practices of well-trained cops,
Devils in the lines of conversation.

Voices brew the hunt for witches who undo
the spell of coffee shops. The night is
fraught with treason. Black cats plot anxieties
you thought you'd turned off like the porch light.
The late leaves shiver. Familiars haunt
the sexless breasts at Hooters.
They carve the headless heads as
frost pulls on its glossed Gestapo boots.
The hand that razors apples
seems to know you.

TERRY HENSEL

The Gutter

I never really believed
I belonged in an elevated world.
I saw myself in the gutter.

I lay in a field at fifteen,
twirling, dancing with Five
Star brandy, my true love.

We laughed and hooted,
until I dreamed and remembered
the dance no more. In my

forties, I envisioned
myself as an alone,
old man padding across

linoleum. Now, here
I am, not yet old, looking
for work, writing proposal

after proposal, while men
are under my house removing
worn, torn, drooping insulation

and installing new,
twice-as-thick insulation.
It's shit work,

dust is everywhere.
I hear them choking
and gagging through

the cheap respirators
I bought them. They're
my crew, skilled craftsmen,

they deserve, and are used to,
better, but construction
is down, and I'm upstairs

estimating projects,
writing proposals,
trying to keep me, and them,

out of the gutter.

The State of the Birds, 2001

Circa 2011

Ill timbre in the trees kept the birds moving,
a restless wind, no perch was safe.
The airborne malcontent
moved through their lofty haven
with ruffled feathers
scattering peace with the blown leaves
and the beauty of their morning songs
became as clanging gongs.

Across our nation, this timbre
of malfeasance sings on either
side of the Avenue,
on either side
of the bed. Good folk, do-right-
by-your-neighbor folk, on either
side of the Avenue, on either side
of the bed, square off
as ruffled grouse flaring red.

There is not peace
where discontent and mistrust nest.

GRAHAM HILLARD

Minor Prophet

I dreamed this and wrote it down,
says the crazy vet
who approaches me on the street,
his feet apart as if braced against God.
He is my father's age. I take
the slip of paper from his rusted fingers.
He is urgent. *What is this word?*
The forest of his script
has not been pruned. An *x*.
An *m* or three broken *t*'s.
A mess of augury. He will not
leave. The spirit is upon him.
Do you know it?
His hands are shaking.
Do you know it?

I don't. His revelation
has been specific. I leave him
in crumbling penitence. The city beyond
is Nineveh. Somewhere
he is carrying out his orders.

Huntingdon, Tennessee: Age 20

The knowledge that we will do nothing
sits on the table between us, gets into the taste

of our eggs and toast, our discussion
of last night's movie and the things

we will accomplish today. And the wall says
I'll beat the shit out of you

if I hear that shit again motherfucker,
and the wall pulses for a moment, the wall braces for

the body it's come to expect, the force
of how much weight we don't know—we've

never seen either of them.
We come home late.

And we chew while the other side
of the duplex has its usual morning.

Forty-five minutes to Jackson by car.
Time to get moving.

H. EDGAR HIX

The New Poor

You can tell the *nuevo pobre* by their inability to stand in lines.
To sit on hold. To fill out the wrong forms three times.
To read old magazines in crowded waiting rooms
or just sit there because no entertainment is provided.
The *nuevo pobre* expect to have names
that professionals will remember.
They expect to see professionals instead of paras.
They think writing a letter from their address does some good.

Their tastes are still for the brand new,
brand name, baked fresh today.
They still think paycheck, not knowing
that dignity is behind them. Not knowing
sleeping with the roaches is the new norm
and the police can tell your accounts are overdrawn.

KAREN PAUL HOLMES

Are Tattoos the New Birthday Suit?

This season, hot pink is the new black
torn stockings, the new distressed denim
shoulders, the new cleavage.

I know ageless is the new age
but if sixty is the new fifty
does that mean I'm forty-five?
Or does the ratio decrease, then reverse
so that twenty-two is the real twenty-two
one is the new three
and babies attend school in the womb?

Though how do you conceive
when instant messaging is the new dating?
Computer games are the new sport, new school
Google, the new library
Twitter, the newspaper.

Is China the New World?
Is Homeland Security our new freedom?
Are banks the new dinosaurs?
And if soy is the new milk,
are soybeans the new cows?

If so, I'll accept the status quo.
Saddlebags might not be the new sexy thighs
nor gray hair the new red
but fifty-five allowed me to move
from the mainstream to the mountains
where trends come slow
and white-faced calves munch on hillsides.

PAUL HOSTOVSKY

Leveling the Playing Field

Before they leveled the playing field
one side was always running uphill,
which was hard. And the other side
was always running downhill, which was
hard too—hard to stop the ball from rolling,
hard to stop yourself from running
when you're running down a hill after a ball.
Downhill had certain advantages though.
It was true. But uphill had advantages too—
you could belay; you could stick a strategic
foot out, trip a careening downhill guy
mid-stride. And anyway, we usually
switched at halftime. So when the referees
came up with the idea, we scratched our heads
and tried to envision a playing field that was
level. "You mean get rid of the hill?" we asked
incredulously. They nodded vehemently
and their excellent silver whistles hanging
on lanyards round their necks bobbed in sympathy.
The bulldozers and the backhoes arrived
the next day, the tines of their buckets biting
into our hill, eating it away before our eyes,
and before we could say time out, or foul play,
or off sides—which some of us did say, although
by then it was too late—they'd gone and changed
the game forever. Some of us quit outright, preferring
to sit in judgment up in the stands—the closest thing
to a hill that they had. And some of us kept on playing,
adapting ourselves to the changing landscape,
learning the new steps, and the new names, making
new friends, many of whom were so young that
they'd never played on a hill. They could only
imagine, they said. They could only shake their heads
and regard us in a squinting sort of way, as though
the sun were going down behind a hill, behind us.

Customer Service

Hello. It feels so good to get a live person.
Let's have a conversation about the weather
in Boston, or Bangalore. I want to talk about
anything except the reason for my call. I'm
sick of me and my problems. Let's talk about you.
Tell me what you see when you look out your window.
Tell me what your hands are doing right now.
Do you know that song by Jim Croce
about lost love and a telephone operator?
Doesn't this feel a little like that song? Keep
talking, please, I love your accent. Yes, I believe
in God. But I don't think God created the world or
even knows we're here. I think the world is a kind of
dream we're having fast asleep in Heaven. Yes, I'll hold...
Hi again. You know, I've been thinking, spiritual texts
are the most boring books in the world—I mean none of them
mentions a bicycle, or a Ferris wheel, or ice cream or baseball
or sea lions. They just lump them all together into the world.
But Heaven is here. Heaven is now. Have you read
any books by Jhumpa Lahiri? Isn't she wonderful?
If this call is being monitored for training purposes,
I'd like to say to all the trainees: just be yourself.
And remember to be human. And remember to be amazed
at how close to each other we sound
when you consider we're a world away.

Lessons on Election Day

On Tuesday we might
dissect a squid.
A squid is an invertebrate.
It's squishy and has
an outer protective shell
called an exoskeleton.
It has a mantle and a jet
propulsion.
It's a mollusk.
Mollusk is a phylum.
There are lots of species
in a phylum
but there are only 8 phyla
in the whole thing,
and California has the most
popular people
because they're worth
55 electoral votes,
and to be the president
you have to be born
in America,
and you have to go
to an electoral college,
and you have to have
a spine.

Foreclosure

We took it out back
and we beat the stuffing out of it,
then we stuffed it, broken, into the back
of the car, and dumped its mutilated body at the dump.
It felt good to do this. After all, the cat had peed on it twice,
and the mortgage company had sent another threatening letter,
and we felt like kicking the shit out of some bankers—
but all we could do was sit back down
on the couch, and drink another beer,
and our helplessness smacked of
cat piss.

So we dragged it outside
and bludgeoned it with the sledgehammer.
Then we took the axe to its back, its arms and legs
and middle, the springs coiled up inside like large and small
intestines spilling out in the yard as we chopped and hacked,
breathing hard from the hard work of beating
the crap out of something you might have
caressed in another life, or another
house, one without a cat with
a urinary tract infection,
or one without

an adjustable rate mortgage,
an ARM you want to break but can't—
so you look around for something else to break,
and it could be your banker or it could be your cat or it could be
someone you loved in another life, or maybe even in this life.
And it feels good to do this. But then it begins
to feel like an indiscretion. And then
like a desecration. And then
it begins, like a death—
a death with its own
life.

JOSEPH HUTCHISON

The Greatest Show on Earth

The clown car careens into the bright-lit
center ring, buzzing like a baby chainsaw.
Smoke corkscrews from the tiny tailpipe,
the horn bleats and squalls. Now it brakes,
fishtails, skids sideways and heaves to a halt,
rocking on lackadaisical springs. The motor
pops and sputters, the tinted glass doors

stay shut. The audience leans forward.
Nothing happens—only spotlight beams
sweeping over, away and back. And soon,
frustration crackles in the bleachers. Gripes,
scattered curses, threats. Nothing happens!
Inside the car's a motley gaggle of eager
Armageddonites, ex-CIA think tankers,

talk radio megastars, flaks for Big Oil—
all playing rock, paper, scissors. The victor
gets to clamber out and take first crack
at deceiving the crowd. Oh, how abashed
they'd be to find the Big Top almost empty!
Just a few gloomy diehards left, their eyes
and nostrils stung raw by exhaust, lungs

too choked for cheers. Imagine the rest
headed home: toddlers riding their parents'
shoulders, the older kids kicking leaves,
all gazing up past bare birch branches
into the red-shifting heart of inexhaustible
openness, the profusion of its forms, feeling
small and glad in the star-spangled night.

Opinions

December 13, 2003

We have the tyrant in custody now—
the one who asked his staff for opinions,
then took one who spoke up next door
and put a bullet in his brain. It's true,

he poisoned whole villages—we've all
seen the pictures: bodies in the dust,
the festival of flies. In that war, though,
the tyrant was our friend, so our protest

came down to a wink, a grin. We said,
"In our opinion, you're still the big man."
Later he got out of hand, of course; seems
he never quite grasped our mission's

virtue, our love of freedom, the size
of our guns. Well, that's all done:
the tyrant's caged now, counting his lice,
crushing each one with a cracked thumbnail;

the reporters' voices stink of triumph. But
what about that boy whose arms our bombs
blew off, whose family we rubbed out: what
is his opinion? And what about our own

dead sons and daughters? Unlike those
who sent them to war—who stayed at home
puffing Cohibas and counting their votes—
our dead remain silent on the subject.

Leaving the Financial District

He's trying to catch the five-forty bus,
walking fast, head down as always,
counting the sidewalk seams as he goes
and pondering the adhesiveness of shadows.

    Up ahead a suspicion sneaks
    black-cat-like across his path.

In his chest a feral tail bristles.
His feet imitate stones.
He sways in place....

    His gaze drifts upward
    across the high-rise cliff-sides. So:
    life's no benign, bewildering dream;
    it's a web traversed by stealthy powers.
    He feels the stare of faceted eyes,
feels the plump abdomens dragging;
venom glitters on fangs like pretty dewdrops,
or blood diamonds, or evening stars.
    And a rough whisper brushes him:
tumblers ticking in a vault's steel door, or old
robed men murmuring oaths of office
(a faint scent of cordite clings to their skin).
    The gutter beside him brims with fluid
murky as film noir blood; leaves
sweep past, their crushed faces whirl,
the current soundless as huddled
children on porches of foreclosed homes,
hugging their knees under boarded windows.

    The choked throat of his wallet throbs.

But he tucks his head, moves on,
obsessively counting the sidewalk seams:
    one, two, three...

while his shadow sloshes at his feet
   like muddy water washing
   to and fro in a gold miner's pan.

JASON IRWIN

Some Days It's a Love Story

At P & G Grocery the dairy manager
has a Bachelor's in Economics
and a pulled groin
from lifting crates of milk.
He's been writing the first chapter to a novel
for six years.
Some days it's a love story,
some days a comedy,
about people in a small town,
like the guy in aisle eight who fits
all he learned from his father
into his right hand and smacks his son
for asking too many questions,
or the cashier at express
who flirts with the younger bank teller
who comes in every day for lunch;
handing him change she smiles,
avoids his eyes and remembers
it's been over two years
since she's been kissed.
Outside, a factory worker, fresh
off the midnight trick,
climbs into a beat-up *Chevy,*
opens a can of *Milwaukee's Best*
he bought for breakfast, takes a sip,
sets it between his legs, keys the ignition
and thinks about the day his wife left,
complaining *he* was the one
who changed.

Cadillacs

Devout as priests, far enough
from their youth to bemoan
the changing times,
these working men—
sons of Sisyphus—toil
in the purgatory of
Monday through Friday, men
hard as gravel, shredded and torn,
fingers gone, stripped like old bolts.

Men like my father, who talked
about *Some Day* as if
it were an actual date
like Christmas or the 4th of July.
Some day, he'd say,
when I save enough money
I'm gonna tell 'em
where they can shove it. Fuck 'em.
Thirty-five years for a watch
and hip surgery.

I see these men at night in diners
and bars, hunched and quiet, faces
cracked, bloodless, unused to sun
or smiles, read the papers,
playing numbers. Men broken
by the promises of a good, hard
day, promises made by men
without mortgages or used cars,
men with soft hands.

After last call they wander
the car dealers' with heavy feet
and lovesick eyes,
groping the Cadillacs
they will never buy.

ROSHANDA JOHNSON

Freestyle on Facebook

I am from unmarked graves and trenches
Where Crips Crypt walk across Crime Street
I take the Number 6 going in the direction of Nowhere
And get off at Hopelessness
I am from the Projects with no rubric
The place where standards sit by and watch
Poverty runs Progress out of the neighborhood
I am from Meth made in Minute Maid bottles
Here we roll blunts with our bucket lists
Here we know better than to believe
Here we don't go to sleep to dream
I am from where Hell scorches High water
Where the view from the high rise is the pavement
And the higher the skirt the better the view of your self esteem
I am from blood
Here nobody sweats your tears
I am from a place where bold means shoot blindly
Where life is like a Vick's Vapor
And you'll get rubbed out by a cold heart
I am from NO NEWS equals no coverage
Cops don't come here and when they do
They leave running
I am from water heated on stoves
Here heartbeats are shared like Cable connections
And lifelines severed and split like veins of Siamese twins

LAWRENCE KESSENICH

Hazardous Materials

> *Adnan al-Sayegh upset the militia, and after reading was*
> *threatened with having his tongue cut out and with death.*
> —*Note on Iranian poet's chapbook cover*

Each time I mail a sheaf of poems
the clerk asks, "Is there anything dangerous
or hazardous in here?" I'm tempted
to joke, "Not unless you consider poetry dangerous."

But then I think of Adnan in Basra, his poems
exploding like car bombs in the minds of his
conservative countrymen, his flight to London,
his exile in a world of poetry as pastime.

For us, it's all play, metaphors numerous as
cereal brands in a supermarket's fluorescent aisles.
We're free to choose exactly what we say and when.
Imagine a world where words are serious as bullets,
where *when* you read your poems can determine if
you'll ever read again. Would I put my life
on the line? Am I brave enough to bleed for poetry?
These are questions to be asked

in the privacy of your own mind. Like the time I heard
a woman scream down the hall from my apartment
and had to decide if being courageous was as important
to me as knowing I would be sitting there the next
weekend, on the sofa with my coffee and newspaper.

ALAN KING

Brink

In an eastern restaurant where
I won't return, a server became a stone
when asked for a refill on Sprite.
Closing my eyes, my nose remembers

the seduction of turmeric and
mustard seed, my tongue tingles
from the memory of cayenne and rice
flavored with cumin and mint leaves.

In that restaurant where I won't return,
a server brought me half a glass of Sprite.
The sound of glass slammed on a table
might've made me think of gavels.

*Everyone knows black people
demand high but tip low*, a friend says.
The owner's expression dark as a judge's robe.
If I closed my eyes, I might've thought

of courtrooms where everyone that looks
like him fills the jury. What my nose and mouth
once knew disappears in a kind of amnesia.
If I closed my eyes while the stone-faced

judge and jury argued me down,
I could've been in a faraway city—
a dot on the atlas of memory—
bordered by what still lingers.

ROBERT S. KING

Cleaning Up

I love the smell of smokestacks in the morning.
I adore the pretty green water where the river
and the pipes meet. It cracks me up to see slick
storks sliding around the beach—love that dark
gooey sand too. I admire the scenery of bald
mountains shaved down to tree stumps. I suck in
the smell of pine tree stacks on logging trucks.
Their black smoke adds just a touch of pepper
to the aroma of this great land.

If you don't like living near the airport, why
don't you move? And don't tell me that everywhere
is in a flight path. Sounds like music to me anyway.
Pretty soon you'll acquire a taste for ambience
and manmade cooking. So stop filtering your
filtered water. Stop complaining about mind
pollution and TV's radiation. That's just white
noise to help you sleep. Just take a stiff drink
and laugh at the news.

I took to global mutation like a duck to oily water,
love its moles and warts without condition.
What man has made has made me rich, won contracts.
I mop up all this dirty beauty and feel blessed
when it comes back. I take a deep breath, think
this is where I'm going to clean up.

Pollyanna Puts on Her Face

In a not-so-bad world powered
by mass-produced miracles
and towers higher than she can count,
she tries to diet her way to the top
where tempers and temperatures
are controlled, blue suits seem so cool,
yet she is so hot.

She works on the 30th story
beneath the AC vent roaring like a plane,
beneath a ton of gravity-defying make-up,
behind a whitened smile tight as a frown.
She reads her not-so-good paycheck as not so bad.

She hums with the muzak.
The company water bottle gurgles
some gossip that's not so bad.
The Fox news channel shouts
some real journalism from the break room.

Standing over her,
the boss's breath is not so bad
when it whispers about a raise
if her output goes up
and her numbers crunch well.

Both he and she watch her figure.
Not so bad, her daily spa waistline
allows a sweet tooth now and then,
but her diet pie in the sky,
like the sugar daddy she seeks,
never quite satisfies.

Perhaps from caffeine, her eyes
seem a little wider these days.

They're getting steamed by the coffee,
her usual warm and fuzzy blend today
brewed hot, just below
the boiling point.

After the War, the War

Since I came home limping, another unknown soldier,
I've lived behind enemy lines.
I guard my homeland now from the front porch
of a house overgrown with undergrowth.

It's jungle-hot and crowded in my mind.
Even cold showers respray the Mekong
in a monsoon of water shadows and attacking waves.
The tub fills with floating bodies,
and the ears fill with bullets thumping flesh.

I want to know if death is victory,
if life is just something you take.
A drunk private, I never heard the war was over.
Fully loaded, my safety is off. A finger curls
around the trigger pulse; the heart beats hard
in the crater of my temple. But I stay on guard,
one eye spotting helicopters, the other hummingbirds;
one ear listening to the sweet work of bees,
the other to the gurgling cries for help.

Old flower children walk by, bent over
and wilted, slow now to remember or care.
Tattoos on bikes pass without mufflers,
their backfires breaking the ceasefire,
my heart backfiring burning blood.
Somehow I go on sweating out my honorably
discharged life, go on in a lukewarm sweat
of shame and honor, a hero who killed for country,
a coward who asked not why his country killed.

I own this house, but I never made it
all the way home. I wander in the mind's wasteland
where the dead are immortal. I watch the leaves
turn orange and burn, watch crows
of black smoke dogfight the hawks.

I march as a blade in a field of grass,
soldiers in formation,
waiting to be mowed down.

Debating the Bibleman

Be careful what you answer,
the bibleman warns me or any stranger.
Not saved? Brother, you're on the low-way to hell.

Preacher, some of us do unto others
better than you who predicts our hell.
If your God is so cruel, you'd better
be careful of what you say in heaven.

Our blood is a mixture of good and bad.
We love and hate; we give and take.

These mean streets fill
with mothers who give because they can,
who labor because they must;
with fathers who lead the blind to shelter
because their spirits suffer with them,
who work because they should;
with sons and daughters taught well
and teaching others.

These are the backbones who try to stand straight,
whose love is not perfect but always freely given,
whose conscience would rather starve than to do harm.

Like me, they are not saved.
Like you, we are far from perfect, but we come closer
than those who would follow
such a mean and shallow God.

JOHN LAUE

Boxes

Most schools are little more
than collections of boxes,
large, small, stacked on one another,
with other boxes in them,
slightly or seriously askew.

In one box is geometry;
in others English,
social studies, P.E.,
foreign languages, art.
Teachers have their boxes too
from tiny mailboxes
in the central offices
to boxes In and Out.

Boxes, hundreds of them,
from morning till late afternoon!
Students move from one box to another
at the sound of bells
like hordes of wind-up soldiers
programmed to their destinations.

When something goes wrong
it's usually because one or more of them
have gotten out of their boxes,
trashed a box,
or because they didn't fit
in boxes in the first place.

Some schools have box police,
laundries, swimming pools,
cafeterias, gymnasiums.
And when students graduate,

teachers retire, administrators quit,
most still live in little boxes,
think in straight lines, checkerboard squares,
never minding that the earth, moon, sun,
heart, stomach, brain prove
nature favors curves and spheres.

SEAN LAUSE

Ashton

Louise's Soda Fountain,
Summer of '62,
the ceiling fan I like to pretend
is a Flying Fortress
stuck there, raging
for death or freedom,
engines churning, round and round.

I'm on my leather stool,
spinning with the Avengers.
There's Louise, her cigarette smoking her,
arm crooked over a jar of "Nigger Babies,"
tiny licorice babies trapped in a jar.
She pops them in her mouth without chewing.
They go down like swallowed hiccups.

And there's my friend, Ashton,
best bunter on the team,
bent on the torn stool,
sitting there for eternities,
touching his ebony elbow,
and staring at that jar
as if the babies are alive.

My uncle's quilt

My uncle cut a swath of his parachute,
strung it like a huge bandage across
his bedroom ceiling. Same memory, each morning.

His B-29. Crashed. They held hands. An oath.
The sharks took them. Just a cry, then
a silence. He alone survived, and told me.

One day he cut it down, that desolate ghost,
and wove it into a quilt of snow
that slowly bled to color, tessellate.

He worked silently, fingers dancing in the wind,
kneading that silk, weaving fields of stars
and a moon, burning like the Paraclete.

I followed its sutures, trails and roads,
secret paths budding to new growth,
a guardian embrace that kept the winds away.

And now, when cold rains nail the earth to pain,
when Winter trees are insect crucifixions,
I sleep beneath all that lonely needle dreamed.

BRENDA KAY LEDFORD

Devastation

Those marketers must have mocked
the hillbillies of Southern Appalachia
as they devised names for subdivisions:
Chestnut Cove, Cherrywood, Hickory Hollow,

Poplar Ridge, Pine Grove, Dogwood Drive,
Sourwood Summit, Smoke Rise, and Eagle View.
Their gimmicks drew greedy developers
to clear-cut the virgin timber,

crush the land of the Cherokee,
destroy the habitat of wildlife.
They leveled the woods,
uprooted the wildflowers,

stabbed the ridges with roads;
mud bled down the hillsides;
the willow trees wept.
Light oozed through the black gum

like bile, creeks reeked with trash,
the Blue Ridge Mountains trembled
as a bulldozer sliced the forest
and ground her bones into dust.

Progress

You know the old logging road,
the one behind the red house,
the one winding past Mama's garden
where morning glories climb the corn;
and you know the path reeks
with trash and broken pines weep
where the loggers butchered trees.

And a mourning dove moans
from the spring where you drew
water for tea and light oozes
through the black gum like bile
as the shadow of a crow passes
over trillium that will soon fade
away like all of us.

You know the Shewbird Mountain
quivers beneath the Thunder Moon
as the mining company
creeps up the mountain
to grind her bones into dust.

LAURA LEHEW

Blocking the ███████ Banner

███ Can you see ███████████
███████████████ twilight's last gleaming?
███ Broad ██████ bright ███████ the perilous fight?
███████ We watch██████ gallantly ██████
███ the rockets██████ the bombs bursting—████
███ proof ██████████████████
██████████ spangled. ██████████
███ Land ██ free █████████ of the brave.█
██████████ Dimly seen, ██████████ the deep█
██████ foe's haughty ██████ silence—████
███████ the breeze██ the towering steep,
███ fitfully blows██ conceals, ██ discloses█
███ catches ██ gleam. ████████████
███ Glory reflected█
██████████████████ may █ wave
O'er the land. ██████████████
And where is ████████████████
███ the havoc of war and ██ battle's confusion?
████████ A country should leave us ██████
Their blood, ████████ their foul ███████ pollution.
No refuge ████ save ██████████
██████████ flight or the gloom of the grave:
███ star-spangled ██████ triumph ██████
O'er the land ████████████ of the brave.
█ Thus be it ever ██████████████
Between ██████ homes and the war's desolation;
Blest with ██████ peace█████████████
Praise ██ Pow'r ████████████████
Then conquer. We must████████████
██████████████████
██████████████████ triumph ████████
O'er the ██████ free and the ██████ brave!

JEAN THURSTON LIEBERT

Letter to Thomas Alva Edison

Dear Sir,

I don't mean to complain.
  You deserve all your fame.
Your light bulb is a work of art.
  In earth's drama it plays a part.

However, not too long ago,
  I solemnly swear this is so,
I visited your laboratory
  and was told this story:

The lightbulb glowing overhead
  Was your very first bulb, they said,
Made with your sweat and tears.
  It's been "on" for 100 years.

Why do I have to jettison
  A bulb every month, Mr. Edison?
Having lived 90 years on this land,
  In a one room house, that's a grand.

It may be too late to fix,
  But you should know of this glitch.
Someone, somewhere, has undermined
  Your wonderful gift to mankind.

Sincerely,

  Concerned citizen

ANDREW SHATTUCK MCBRIDE

I am no different

Dedicated to Nathaniel Anthony Ayers, Jennifer Ayers-Moore
and the Ayers Family

I. Present

Across the green a man shouts at no one and everyone,
"OK, I'll repeat it again: I f***ing give up. I'm done."
He is animated and loud. He is ragged,
and next to him there is a bag, but no cart.
There are few people: we hurry by, keeping to this side
of the green; some veer away entirely.
We become interested in the ground, or in the buildings
nearby, or in the bronzed statue
of the town's founder. We retreat into ourselves
as if everything is normal. Seeking our own comfort,
we do everything but that which is right.

I am no different.

II. My Past (1973)

In Honolulu, at the 'A'ala Park bus stop, a man shouts
at the top of his lungs. It isn't English. It is a single
word—sounding like an urgent "Battabah!"—shattering
conversations. The man is intense and wiry, and he
roams a place dense with waiting people. Others begin
sneaking glances. Every few minutes he yells the word
again, over and over but from different places within
the crowd, punctuating the wait.

I am startled at his first shout. At his second shout,
I work hard at not laughing; I do not want this man's attention
on me or on my girlfriend. Jené looks at me in silence.
We are teenagers, and in the islands we are haoles.
She is a California girl, from the Bay area. I am a

local boy, from the Big Island. Honolulu and its crowds
challenge me, and I have never seen so many people.

The word might be Filipino, but I don't recognize it
in pidgin. I have no answers. "Battabah!"
he shouts, again and again. We retreat into each
other, ourselves. Does he leave first? Do we?
When we board a bus, relief washes over us.

Later that same year Dad gives me the harmonica
I've asked for. I like the sounds it makes, but
I'm not adept. In the new year, I finally put it away,
without learning how to play.

III. Recent Past (2007)

Foreclosure. When I "lost" my house I knew the streets
were suddenly closer. While I had enough,
without a house the homeless became immediate to me.
I observed closely, learning.

I am no different.

IV. This Present

I view the ragged, dirty man and the woman and child
on a bench nearby. In their expressions
I see the hardness of days; in hers wariness and the
fear of nights. Yet, in seeing the way she holds her child
I know that love and mothering have not failed here.

His tattered jacket is mine. Her shapeless clothes shield me.
This toddler's eyes give me new sight for the world.

I am no different.

V. Future

I turn away from the person who I once thought I was.
I have no pity, but what is emerging

is compassion and empathy. Curiously,
with less owned, I have time—and more—to give.

When I see her again, I will make sure she knows—
and finds—Agape, a shelter for women and children.

In the meantime, the green is deserted.
I ease slowly toward the man.
Today he is not shouting. He looks at me.
"Mister, what do you want?" His words are crisp.
"Don't give up." My voice is like a frog's croak.

"What do you want? I don't have any drugs."
What do I want? Nothing. No, everything. To help.
I look at him. Questions race through my head:
Can I help? Does he know about the Mission?
Can I take him there? Has he eaten?

"May I sit down?" He nods warily,
gesturing at the bench nearby.

I take out the harmonica I've
brought. He watches me, impassively. I ask
"Do you know how to play?"
"Harmonica? No, but I wouldn't mind learning."
I nod, "Me too."

I am no different.

I hand the harmonica to him. His hand is hard,
callused, with nails outlined in dirt. He wipes the
harmonica with a clean cloth which he has produced
somehow, magically. Experimenting, he blows a riff.
It is a harsh but rich, beautiful sound.

We smile.

We are no different.

JIM MCGARRAH

Interstate 24

I'm forty-nine miles from Chattanooga
stumbling through the radio in my old Toyota
searching for noise to take away the ceaseless buzz
of tread-bare Goodyear tires. Like a shark,
inertia drives me crazy. I decide a burred bearing
will cure monotony and settle on a female preacher
who says, "Beer is the real problem" & I think of Jesus,
his blanched bones scattered, his soul in a make believe
place, his flesh desiccated so our apathy matters.
Jesus—wanting only a draft or two of Pabst Blue
after a hard day with hammer & nails & blisters
trying to carpenter something solid, yet knowing
nothing of how to build paradise. Then, cousin John
coaxes him to a stream, holds his head under water,
deprives his brain of air till god appears as a dove.
That's when Jesus ends up hung on a stake, a carcass
of transubstantiation so the rest of us can feed on his misery
with Inquisitions & Crusades, jihads & dead Jews,
televangelists who love meth & priests who love little boys.
We can't even get ourselves born
without committing some original sin. Suddenly,
a message comes to me in a blinding flash of lights
from an oncoming semi, kinda like what happened
to old apostle Paul & caused him to fall off his mule
on the road to Damascus. This radio lady's bat-shit crazy
and, no lady, beer ain't the *real* problem.

Elegy for Charles Darwin

on the 150th Anniversary of The Origin of Species
and During the Trial of Faith Healer Dale Neuman

He reasoned we'd evolve,
become greater than the sum of our parts,
but Darwin never met Dale,
who killed his daughter with prayer
because doctors are devils.

He conjectured we'd adapt
from the inside, like Stop Leak,
and plug the holes in our lives,
bar our souls from oozing out,
check ignorance from seeping in.

Darwin surmised we'd adjust
to our futures, but Dale didn't like
this new century full of free will,
science minus magic, and no gods left
to exorcise his ten-year-old's diabetic demons.

Dale prayed, injecting spirit instead
of insulin and for his faith, his prayers
were answered. A coma cured his daughter
and sent her back to Jesus, a home where
Darwin's evil is barred from entry.

25 Cents

All the man asked me for
was a quarter,
and here I am tripping.
All caught up in my assumptions
about who he is
where he's been
and what my little 25 cents
or lack thereof
might do
to change his destiny.

The man did not ask for
my opinion.

He didn't ask me to save him
or damn him
all he asked for
was a fraction
of what it costs me to wash one load of clothes
and I ain't even going to the laundrymat today.
I know I lost at least
that much in gas
the last time I filled up
trying to squeeze one last drop
in the tank.

It makes me wonder
what exactly it is
about this man
that makes my little 25 cents
mean so much more to me
just because he asked.

NANCY CAROL MOODY

Liberty

The Statue of Liberty
is standing on a street corner
in Springfield, Oregon.
Her skin is dark as steerage, hair
the colors of a postcard sunset.
The rays of her crown are made of foam.
Her gown, the tempest-tossed green
of every battered shore
this side of Eureka,
ripples from the exhaust of teeming cars,
the wretched commuters huddled,
stuck in 5 o'clock traffic
on Gateway Street.
But she's beaming, our Liberty,
with a smile that spreads from sea
to shining sea, her plastic torch backlit
by the lamp of the IHOP
that takes up half the block. And if
she's tired, it doesn't show:
headphones in ears, she bounces
on the toes of her stars
and stripes shoes, her arm arcing
in great yearning waves, directing
the masses toward the safe harbor
of the parking lot, to the golden door
of Liberty Tax, where their returns
will be calculated, their paperwork filed, where
in forty-five minutes they'll be sent on their way,
one hundred dollars poorer, but breathing free.

American Intrinsic

Amputate the tributary, and the willow
succumbs like chewed taffy. Suckling
the muck-belly of the lagoon: powdered wig,
snippets of parchment, a picnic baseball.

Reflex is contagious: the monkeys
on the bank are waxing collegial, silk
watermarks concealed in their palms,
a pound of intestines bartered for soil.

The airborne scud through the pillows,
fumbling with their ersatz ears.
Abandoned to his hangar, the bald bird
hunkers, his wingspan furrowed.

American Climatic

December: the trees possessed
by the gods of glitz, leaves
and needles singed with warmth.
An insurgence of clouds
gingerly treads the distance.

In this wrinkled moment, not a whiff
of snow in the blear. Rain advances,
satcheled with gloom. Stockings
slacken before the fire, their long
shadows ancient, fuggy as tears.

A perilous daybreak, Christmas,
sodden canary of global waning.
Food and philosophy define
the differential, the cityscape
fraught in the reindeer's mirror.

Roy's Five-and-Dime

Store For Sale

Do you see the signs in front of Roy's Five-
and-Dime? *For Sale,* they say. The whole town knows
Roy. He grew up here, kept business alive.
Do you see the signs? In front of Roy's, five
BB holes have cracked the glass. Stray cats thrive.
Roy's all out of hope; now the store will close.
Do you see the signs in front of Roy's Five-
and-Dime? *For Sale.* They say the whole town knows.

The Way It Used To Be

This is the way it used to be—Dee made
popcorn fresh each morning. The store would fill
with the smell. Hand-drawn signs tried to persuade:
This is the way. It used to be, Dee made
batches, loved to see the kernels displayed.
Now she pours them from bags and thinks, Some skill
this is. The way it used to be, Dee made
popcorn fresh. Each morning, the store would fill.

The Fall Sale

The yardage sale starts today. The bolts of
fabric stitch a rainbow on the back wall.
Outside the store the housewives wait. They love
the yardage. *Sale Starts Today!* The bolts of
cloth will be unrolled; the women will shove
and push in line. It happens every fall—
the yardage sale starts. Today the bolts of
fabric stitch a rainbow on the back wall.

Grinding Keys

It's not very hard—all the clerks can tell
when a man needs a key. Ken sells him two
minutes of time, shares a good joke as well.
It's not very hard. All the clerks can tell
of cranky customers banging the bell.

If Ken wants a fellow to get his due,
it's not very hard. All the clerks can tell:
When a man needs a key, Ken sells him two.

Aisle 9, Pets

Water bubbles in the tanks. Yellow, green
and blue feathers skitter across the cold
floor. Children gape as if they've never seen
water bubbles. In the tanks' yellow-green
world, the fish flitter and dart. The birds preen—
they don't yet know they're about to be sold.
Water bubbles in the tanks, yellow-green.
And blue feathers skitter across the cold.

In Toys

The staff's been laid off; there's no help in Toys.
The kids do what they want to do. *Come back,*
a frantic mother calls, chasing her boys.
The staff's been laid off. There's no help. In Toys,
handless mannequins dressed in corduroys
turn up from Sports, and the checker gets flak.
The staff's been laid off. There's no help. In Toys,
the kids do what they want to. Do come back.

Closing Time

The chrome-railed counters at the five-and-dime—
loaded with pies, shakes, burgers, fries. Boys swoon,
eyeing the girls in pink. At closing time
the chrome-railed counters at the five-and-dime
are scoured with bleach, the day's spatter and grime
stripped by the women who know like a tune
the chrome-railed counters. At the five-and-dime—
loaded with pies, shakes, burgers, fries—boys swoon.

Sweeping the Store

At night Roy Junior sweeps the store, the day
reduced to a pile of dust. He hopes for

luck—loose change on the floor means extra pay
at night. Roy Junior sweeps. The store, the day,
months of days. He filches a Milky Way,
chews the candy as he completes his chore.
At night Roy Junior sweeps the store, the day
reduced to a pile of dust he hopes for.

JANELL MOON

Mystery

The Gay and Lesbian Metropolitan Community Church in
San Francisco lost more parishioners in the ten years between
1983-1993 than any other church in the world.

We grew up with the minister,
watching him bury our dead with compassion
living in his body as prayer, asking for healing
as death comes, as life unfolds,
his blessings given as he himself passes from youth
to middle age infected with the virus.
He asks us to be the sanctuary,
a safe place for the lost, for the loneliness in ourselves.

We're given grief's raveled cloth to repair, each
in our own way. A couple begins
to understand love just as one partner
loses his sight. Another gets better,
now with bills he can never pay,
a trip to India living on in his eyes.
The young man doesn't want his hand empty,
keeps a tissue in his fist, a reminder than God holds him.

There is a bowl set out for each one of us.
I have felt it round and overflowing.
I don't know what will come next,
when the wing of change or chance
will sail through, land at our feet
asking us to bow to our finality.
I do know there is nothing else but living
as I know how, my hand in yours.

GEORGE NORTHRUP

Sedona Experience

Los Abrigados Inn
leaves a bottle of water
in the kitchenette
"for the thirst-quenching
convenience of our guests"
and warns that
"a charge of $6.00 will be added
to your bill upon opening."

Nearby a complimentary tea bag
rests upon a subtle memo
that more are available
at the Resort Gift Shop.

Generous sizes of shampoo
and maximum body conditioner
greet the traveler
at the bathroom sink
with—oops!—a "Special Offer"
to purchase these for $19.95.

On the coffee table lies
a brightly colored magazine,
Experience Sedona,
on every page
an opportunity to spend.
The Dining Experience,
The Lodging Experience,
and, of course,
The Shopping Experience.

Here, in red-rock country,
where the Chamber of Commerce
is said to rest upon a vortex

negative in qi,
where you cannot even
drive back from Safeway
without a mesmerizing view,
experience Sedona
while you can,
before they hang tall curtains
on the canyon walls
and charge your credit card to revel in
The Viewing Experience.

American Materialism: the Rococo Period

Your new dishwasher, as always,
sprays soapy water
at your dirty dishes,
only now the racks adjust,
the interior is stainless,
controls tilt out of sight,
and the sound is whisper quiet.
Are the dishes any cleaner?
That is not the point.

Your new automobile, as always,
advances when you step on the gas,
stops when you step on the brake,
keeps you warm in winter,
cool in summer,
wipes raindrops from the windshield,
lights your way in fog and dark,
only now it holds your cappuccino,
plays music from eight speakers,
throws balloons at you in a crash,
and even when your spouse is absent,
tells you exactly how to drive.

SCOTT OWENS

Conjugal Rites

I was the first she wanted to marry.
No surprise there. Every dad
a daughter's first love. But then
she felt bad about excluding her mom,
decided the three of us should tie the knot.
We had to tell her you only marry one
other person, at least you plan it that way
and mommy and I were already married
to each other. She moved on to first
one brother, then the other, both of whom said
you can't marry your brother. So then
she tried her best friend, a girl, asked
to be clear if girls could marry each other.
Already thrice denied what could we say
to make sense to a four-year-old.
Yes, of course, but only in some places,
only where love is not prescribed by law.

JUDITH PACHT

Falcon

Dunsmuir, Scotland

Never mind *diurnal,* I know

you seize the day, calculate
fly-time to the fraction

of a wink, those unblinking

gold-flecked eyes
measure the hare's gait

from half a mile. Wing-swing, dive,

thunderbolt of notched beak
quick to the back, snapping it.

It's what you dream at night I want to know,

how sleep hones precision:
below, the darkened field of oil seed rape

or gorse, the tremble of a stalk,

the twitching ears, the scurry.
You know the carrion's mind or spine,

how to break each one

precisely—a kind of nocturnal
practice for a clean kill

—not sport, not

human fantasies
splayed,

hooded black

or red on a concrete floor
like those, say

in Abu Ghraib.

CHRISTINA PACOSZ

Four Gates to the City: South

> *If you murder a city, you murder a nation.*
> —*Seva Forrest,* Shopping Bag Ladies

And what, she asks, struggling
to her swollen feet in the cold alley,
the empty gutted storefront, the glaring
fluorescence of the bus station
at 2 AM, what about the self?

She is walking a city
street with her parents and brother
deep in the heart
of summer twilight and the sky
is a bird's egg
of fragile blue-green light.
Air moves on her skin, a gentle mouth.
She runs across the boulevard
dodging the swift and deadly cars.

She is whole, holy
running toward the rib joints
reeking of grease,
running toward the knots
of young men on street corners
and winos pissing on themselves
Yes, she is running in the night
toward the melting ice
and the river, toward
the harsh neon of strip joints,
massage parlors, the pornography
of women selling desperate flesh.
She is running past all threat
and danger, her feet pounding
the hot pavement, the taste
of metal in her mouth.

The emissions of too many cars
and factories and not enough
green room thick in her throat.
The acrid smell of defeat
and disgust in her nostrils
eager to worm its way inward.
She is running toward the bored police,
brutal in their blue uniforms.
She is running past the crowded stoops
of summer, peopled in the humid dark
with the rise and fall of laughter.
The anonymous camaraderie of the city
covers her like a cloak, a benediction.
A blessing.

Murder by the (Wrong) Numbers

My point is that it has to be both: beautiful and political.
I'm not interested in art that is not in the world.
—Toni Morrison

One spring night not long
ago, a barred owl
hooted from the ailanthus tree
outside our window.
Now weaponry of assorted caliber is what I hear

as I try to sleep soundly
enough to dream
and remember.
This past August
a man was found dead in the street.

I heard the shots that killed him
at 56th and Garfield—
three loud pops in a row.
Then, only a few nights ago
another man.

Gunshots and submachine
gun fire, a brief
and deadly duet.
And last night
windows open

to the dark
street, vehicles
at high speed—
maybe cop cars—
but turning over is difficult and painful.

Without my glasses
I can't be certain

but swift cars at 3 AM
tear up and down
the narrow street.

You wake long enough
to ask, "What's wrong?"
Facing east
trying to explain
my unease

as if dawn itself was a menace.
Despite October's chill
the triplet of old windows
is open still.
Our butterscotch cat

a pale shadow
hunched on the edge
of the mattress
gazing east.
At 5 AM

the local station
has Breaking News:
about 2:30 AM
an eleven year old girl was shot sleeping
in her own bed.

Her condition is now upgraded
to stable.
This child's survival
a reply to the lethal greeting
from the predatory street.

LEE PASSARELLA

They Eat the Lean

> *If Americans continue to pack on pounds, obesity will*
> *eat up about 21% of health-care spending.*
> —News item

Remember your Old Testament?
Pharaoh's dream of the seven fat cows,
the seven lean ones? The lean cows eat
the fat: seven years of famine in the wings.

Here in the waiting room of the ER,
reality and logic reassert themselves:
the fat cows finally dine upon the lean.
They trundle in in their wheelchairs,

their ample derrieres larding the seats
lovingly made double-wide to accom-
modate fat-assed America. As they sit
and wait, they appear to be melting,

hauled down by gravity, puddingy-white
with the specter of systems failure. Some sip
oxygen as if it were iced latte, through endless
straws. Behold, they lick the platter clean.

Love's Lexicon

Love always teaches you new vocabularies.
Now, your local, onboard dictionaries
don't count for much; you need to download
custom ones, to cover the new meanings
you've coined for archaisms such as
lip and *breast* and *thigh.* Or to replace
the jaded smirk of four-letter brush-offs
that used to adequately parse those nether
mysteries of which you're now an acolyte.

And when you happen to be in love
with a self-destroyer, you learn
the melodious Latinates of end-stage disease:
ascites—old books call it *dropsy*—
cholestasis—the liver shutting up its shop, for good—
encephalopathy—brain sickness, as unlovely
a thing as its name is purest music,
honeyed stream of round
vowel sounds
and breezy aspirates.

GARTH PAVELL

The Ongoing Conversation

The trees and I are in the park, backs to the Wall Street dream
drained of the long ago yesterday belief that our transactions
set us free. Poised like an improper prayer I imagine it's midnight
and I'm dating a scandalous day trader intern yearning to learn
the relic currencies that ski the interloping slopes of our hopes.
Ah, but it's only March, the Hudson's blue ringlets are chattering
endless escape routes around Lady Liberty's lime. The first days
of spring toss Morse-like crumbs to the elder nights in this
institutionalized era while I surmise if I'm less than light-years from
brilliant love orbiting above our ink that holds in or out the unwritten
secrets of our see-through jar when suddenly a dark long haired girl
sits at the next bench with her invisible traffic light pulsing to yield.
I sense she's not really reading The Economist because let's face it
who is but I inquire anyway if she requires more light. She's shocked
I broke the hermetic seal of silence. And then it's as if we compress
hours of film, become fast-forwarded blooming flowers even though
in actuality we're burning leaves. I smile all kid-like which reveals
the unrecorded kinship of perished ecosystems that somehow still play
in my DNA. Her eyelids curtsy a knowledge I've never known.
I sense she's on the brink of giving me a lift 'round the manmade block
and then to my surprise raises her eyelashes like a camisole and asks if
I think it's going to rain. No, it's the frayed statistics, gumballs of money
expanding and popping from the lubricated crunch of exchanged hands.
At least they're exchanging, she says with the rip and roar of a civilized
war, succumbing to rationalize some deserve astronomically more.
Her face is now like a heretic in a bombed-out potato field searching for
leftovers from a disastrous god decreed no doubt little killing spree
that suggests the ergonomics of dildos go deep within our psyche.
Unfortunately (she points out) when it comes to commerce our philanthropy
is still in the planning stage. Geez, I say, you should get a job as a spokesman
for the conglomerates. Spokesperson, she corrects, raising the periscope
out of my pants. True, the economy's lounging crisis is like a peace march
lethargically stampeding, peeking through the doors of AIG, oh great finance
wonderland booby-trapped with cash. You think derivative swaps were
    mothered

by nurture or nature, I ask. She looks at the water glimmering like a trusted
shoeshine leading down unforeseeable paths. We do what can be done,
    she says,
her smile vaporizing like a summa cum laude attorney crafted getaway
    clause.

JOEL PECKHAM

The Fog

does not descend or drop; it does not
fall. But grows—thickens in the throat,
gathers like the fur of mold. Slips in, holds on,
insistent with the gentlest hands of a lover
or the memory of love. And then, at once, is
everywhere so all the frightened drivers slow
to nothing on the roads we didn't know

we longed for. There is so much
we don't know, and what we do seems
useless. Worse. This sense it all
could be slipped off like silk, lifted away so we,
for once, could see each other floating past
each other. On the loop outside the city,

roadside flares light water, light air, and bloom,
red as tail-lights blinking through the fog.

Sermon

1.

And the people will gather. Having
Come to the Sermon At The Mountaintop
Removal—also called The Sermon By
The Concentrated Animal Feeding Operation
or in some texts referenced equally as
The Sermon At The Elevated Parking
Garage or The Sermon at the Wal-Mart
or the Sermon Where The Plain Used
To Be but no-one will remember where
or what a "plain" was and so will finally
and more accurately be called The Sermon
Over There Where All Those People
Are Gathering...

2.

This blasting rocks the earth, tears
it at the coal-seams. World become
Energy. Peak performance. Yield.
It takes a people (who can see a tree only
for how long it takes to burn) to rip the sky
itself apart. Toxins seep into the rivers
and run off down the mountainside with deer
or float as ash into bird-wheeling absences
of dusk and shadow. And we are long past
no, please don't, and *stop.* Somewhere past
exhaustion when all the soil, stone, and roots
settle into overburden dumped into a holler-
fill or are re-shaped to form the approximate
contours of the mountains, only softer,
throbbing like a bruise. People will return—
perhaps a man sloshing through a river
with a boy. They speak in low tones, listening
for once and before and maybe, new grass
growing on a hill where the valley used to be.

DIANA PINCKNEY

The Coal Bin

after Elizabeth Bishop

The President died today, my friend
Lila tells me, her hand on her heart.
I am seven. It is 1945. A war is
going on. Each night in bed, I replay
my brother's story—*Germans
in our cellar, behind the coal bin*—I whisper
to Lila, who cries when I challenge her

to walk across the hall grate covering
the furnace that heats our house. She's
a little mouse with papery skin and hair, with
pale eyes that water when I describe
submarines under waves thrumming
toward her family's beach cottage, how
at the stroke of midnight, little men
will crawl through dunes to the porch, moonlit
hammocks creaking. Lila vows not to go

this summer or ever. Opening the cellar
door, my father starts down
to stoke the furnace. *Ridiculous,*
he answers when I ask about
the enemy below. *Stop your foolishness,*
Mother says, bending to the radio's
wooden arc that drums of battles, each
day's news attended to, each night's blackout
secured by shades dark as Father's slick black

coat and hat he wears out the door,
an air-raid warden on rounds. Tonight, after
he hangs his hat on its rusty porch hook,
after the house clanks and groans

into sleep, I dare myself downstairs
to the hallway. The furnace rumbles—
Step on me—commands—*do it*—
one leap over the hot grate—
I'm on the other side.
It is 2012. War is going on.

KENNETH POBO

Oh That's So

gay, she says, referring to my
salmon-colored short-sleeve shirt,
which my brother told me
to stop calling a "top,"
boys don't wear tops,
we wear shirts, and evidently

it's very, very gay to say
"This is my salmon-colored
short-sleeve top." She doesn't

hate me or the shirt (top,
if you prefer), but for her
life is a bologna sandwich—
bread (gay),
bologna (straight)
and she prefers not to think
about the butter. Her coat,

wool and golden, but I
can't figure out
its sexual preference, and

she has already gone on
to the secretly bisexual
food court.

DAVID RADAVICH

Stars and Strife

We do love our guns.

Is it the penis-like action
that excites, hard

extension
of our manhood,

or the unitary
sensation of casting

off the other
we would rather die

than deal with?

America's little secret:
death is the best
lover, more

reliable than sex
or race-cars or even nature

that can be taken away
with one bullet.

Wrap your arms
around that final flag.

Foreclosure

A lone voice
echoes in the woodwork,

delicate fingers
of rain

tap
on the window—

history, desire, oppression
that once made their home here

still in the walls

under the paint

cry out
for release

ache
for justice

if only we could hear
the ancestors

of air

M. S. ROONEY

Memorial

There are many facts
about the Vietnam
War Memorial Wall:
how the artist was chosen,
the number of names and the number of slabs,
the reason the highest point of the stone
is the highest.

But I remember this:

That the wall looked to me
like the sharp angle of an old coffin,
the kind you can slip a body from
feet first,
the kind you can use
again and again.

That I found the one I knew
would be there.
Line number, slab number,
his place in this order
of things.

That I did not find the one I feared
would be there.

That the book of names was soft and worn.

That I ran my finger
again and again over the list,
so many
with his same uncommon
last name.

LINWOOD RUMNEY

Some Lullabies

On the second floor our neighbor
is beating his girlfriend again
while their child screams.
She begs him to leave the boy
alone. I know you have probably
heard this story before,
so I won't trouble you with details
of late night calls to police
and his promises
to break clean.
                    I am ten. Tonight
I have wet the bed again, risen
and showered, pulled the sheets
from the stained mattress
and flopped onto the couch
in my mother's bathrobe.
                              Strange
though it may seem, the rhythm
of this beating—the syncopated
thumps, the blunt bass of his fists
on her body or the wall, the child's
strained alto grown hoarse—all of this
lulls me back to sleep. Like you,
I've heard it before, but I know
that in a few hours they will tire
of this violence.
                      I'll stir only
when my mother comes home
and presses her cold hand
to my forehead. It reeks
of raw herring she gutted
and canned all night at the factory.
I pretend not to notice that she trembles,

not from worry, but the routine
of exchanging her strength
for a paycheck.
                    As she turns
from me, sprawled on the couch
and pretending to sleep, she will say
nothing of the damp sheets beside
the hamper. In this way
we grant each other the privacy
of our distinct shame.

TINA SCHUMANN

A Day in the Life

It is 8 a.m. and everyone is waiting
for their lives to begin. We have made it
through the bad machinery of night
and now await the conundrum of another day.

With backpacks and satchels full
of hypnotic calculations we walk
like accidental anthems with hands
in pockets to bus stop and office,

our usual seat before the podium.
Now some small manifesto
of self emerges, another way
to proclaim our aim, reiteration

of mandate and mantra.
Soon it is 12 p.m. and the clock
has cut the day in half.
Now a respite from the morning

grind, now a downhill slide. Before we know it
it is 4 p.m. and everyone is waiting
for the day to end. With a slowing of the breath
and a cooling of the skin, every gesture a rendered amen;

the pen finally laid down, the phone ignored,
each chair rolled neatly to its given slot.
With eyes firming in their gaze and a gait
adjusting to the evening routine—

we have carried ourselves well,
contained the troublesome boundaries
of the body and surrendered,
yet again, to a rendition of one.

A World of Want

You think your life will go on
like this forever; weekly trips
to the garbage bin, untangling
the green snake of hose between the ferns
and the delphiniums, the coral bells
leaning their long necks
against the back fence.
Today, as I watched
the carousel of cars
turn one by one through
the intersection and onto
the freeway I tried to imagine
each life. Not so much where they were
going, but what they were made of:
wounds, illusions, desires, deceits...
Through all of this a preoccupation
with the next perceived need floats up
like thought bubbles inside my head:
Coffee, Cheetos, sex, a new blouse, a larger house, recognition,
a desk fan, appreciation from that one specific person,
the phone's chirp, the trip to France.
If I could quiet this conga-line of cravings,
what lingering longings would I lament?
What radiant unattached insights
would I muster? Who would I be
without my constant yearnings?
It's a world of want. You get the idea.

ERIC PAUL SHAFFER

Ellipti City

I've lived in this city my whole life, and there ain't nothing wrong
with this damned place. Our monuments are magnificent, all white marble,
pointy and perfect as anything earthly that aspires to sky.

The streets run one way sometimes, sometimes both ways. Hell,
you got to look for the signs and arrows. We have local bars at mid-block

on every boulevard and churches on every corner. There are plenty
of good schools and jails, and even more malls. Banks are everywhere,
and there are sidewalks for the homeless to sleep on. You can dine

on the world's finest cuisine within fifty square miles of the capital building.
Highways are broad, and every single driver takes the beltway to a job
he's glad to have. This city was built for eternity. The founders leveled

forests and drove the trunks into the mud. They raised rotundas and galleries
and libraries and built offices infinite and obscure, making us the envy

of the free world. You don't have to tell me again the streets are sinking
into the swamp on which it stands. This is a city of dips and slants and angles.
George's Obelisk tilts seven degrees from true, but the tip still points at the
    sky.

If there's a slope in every federal floor and ceiling, it's nothing we can't
    ignore.
We're secure in pomp and circumstances. We're thirteen miles from the
    ocean,
so I never worry about tidal waves, or earthquakes, or volcanoes or floods

neither. I ain't never seen one and never will. This city can take whatever
wickedness the weather throws at us. Our river is broad and brown, but the
    levees

are high, and they've held for nigh on two hundred years. Our sky is brown,
    too,
but look at that sunset over the skyline. Every night, the western clouds burn
on the dark horizon, and our city is framed in gold and scarlet flames.

The Red House in Washington

Well, Wolf, the president himself has said very little
about the rising death toll in Iraq since that speech of his,
now almost two months ago, in which he declared
major combat operations over.
—John King, CNN

"John? I'm sorry. We seem to have lost our uplink with John King due to local transmission problems. We'll pick up our live report later. We take you now to the White House which has been repainted a remarkable new color—blood red. Our Washington Fashion Correspondent Janey Bobainey discusses the flaming bright colors that are in for the summer season. Janey, I can see behind you the White, I mean, the Red House in all its new glory, but I have to say that paint is conspicuously darker than I expected. It looks suspiciously like dried blood. What can you tell us about that?"

"That's right, Wolf. When wet, the paint is bright fire-engine red, but drying changes the hue considerably. This is the color the President himself chose. He is a close friend of the Corporate President of Home Despot, warehouse supplier of home destruction materials as far East as the Middle East. The President imported special ingredients from the battlefields of Iraq, and the color will be available to the public by Fall as 'Burnt Crimson.'"

"Just in time for the autumn leaves to turn."

"Another bold decision declaring the President's resolve as we move toward the November elections."

"Yes, those natural reds are most striking. Brilliant reds, simply brilliant."

"Breathtaking, indeed."

MARIAN KAPLUN SHAPIRO

Annual Pigeon Shoot, Higgens, PA

This morning, Labor Day, the news
at seven finds me half-listening,
waiting for the promised
habañera of Bizet, and later
for a new orchestral Gaité
Parisienne. A bomb has caused
'collateral damage' somewhere
in the Middle East (that means
that children have been killed).
Florida warns its residents:
the con men are slithering
in the wake of the looters
across the path of rubble
of the first Fall hurricane. *Of course.*
What else? Soon Bizet. Then Offenbach.
But one more item before
the weather for Boston and vicinity
(*will it warm up enough*
to have the usual barbecue?)
From Higgens, Pennsylvania, we learn,
the annual pigeon shoot is underway.
(*People shooting pigeons? Well, perhaps*
they are a plague, a Tiananmen Square
of raucous birds, carriers of disease...)
The newscaster continues: The way
it's done, he says, is fixed by ritual.
Crammed into crates, the birds
are starved. Thus, a very few
can fly when freed. Those get away.
The others are shot down. Presumably,
it doesn't take too long. Plenty
of time to picnic. Probably
the winner gets a prize. This year
there are a few protesters,
bussed in from New York.

The mayor is annoyed. New York, of all
places! People should learn
to tend to their own back yards!
Mind their own business, and leave
each to his own.

MICHAEL SHORB

Touch My Junk and I'll Have You Arrested

Beware of the aroused
American, he's taken
quite a load on himself
already, agreeing to
phase out social security,
work until 70,
donate more time
to the needy, which includes
most of us.

We don't speak here
of Daniel Boone
using his knife
to elbow a bear
from an oak tree,
we don't evoke
a bearded fur trapper
bathing naked
in some icy stream,
puffing on his pipe
with a whiskey smile.

Just leave me
the 60-inch screen,
the vision phone holding
the sum of my life,
the freedom to open
a bank account or
a refrigerator,
and if I really do
need to revisit
whatever fragment of family life
I feel compelled by,
make the line I stand in small,
and whatever the
hell you do, don't touch my junk.

NANCY SIMPSON

First Responder

I was the first to arrive
though bystanders stood
immobile. My legs wouldn't move
but my training stepped forth.

My arms reached out.
My hands dug through rubble
that smoke-filled day.
I raised bodies. In the night

my lungs gave out. Now
you want all I know.
I can't recall one name, not even
the face of a brother who worked at my side,

his arm and my arm pulling forth a woman, alive.
I remember her scream and thought
touched by terror what happened to her
will keep happening for the rest of her life.

That's not enough. You want more?
Will you think me shallow-minded if I tell you
that day, until my last breath, I heard
the sound of cell phones ringing.

RON SINGER

Listen Hard Enough

(for Butchie Maxwell)

The quiet seems absolute
but, if you listen hard enough,
you can hear children's voices
from the other side of the world.

It is a beautiful day,
weather "like it used to be."
Clouds roll through a dark-blue sky,
wet snow in a dogless city,
so white, so heavy, so clean.

The wind, of course, you can hear
without trying. Crickets, birds, too.
But, if you listen hard enough,
certain sounds from deep in the woods
seem a mingling of children's voices.

Picture these kids, if you will,
begging, selling petty goods,
running in and out of traffic
on a teeming African street,
or perched high on a garbage hill
in the heart of some *favela.*

One looks up, perhaps, and sees
wet-white clouds in a dark-blue sky
and, who knows, he may be listening
to you. He hears your distant heart.

J. D. SMITH

Country Data

The lingua franca is English in most regions.
All beverages are in some way made with oil.

Meat consumption remains high among the lower classes,
whose dogs subsist on scraps mixed with grain.

Imports include but are not limited to
manufactures and debt,

while entertainments and cash crops represent
the leading exports

in spite of thinning topsoil
and hope.

On the Amish

My days measured in emails,
pressed through spreadsheets,
I imagine joining the Plain People
of barn-raisings and broad-brimmed hats
in the fields amid horses of sturdy use.
After decades of gasoline and electric gears,
there's little left to miss before entering
an idyll where a tool need not drown out speech
because there is, in fact, all day to do the job
every day save the Sabbath.
Because there is nowhere that needs going to
until the market, not a concept but an event,
there to meet those with soft hands
whose joints now creak too much
to bail hay or milk a cow
but like to know that someone still does,
who have tested microwave and laptop
and found them good, like insurance.
They are called the English,
like me, who palm uncounted change into a pocket
and hope, across a table and a world, to shake hands.

M. R. SMITH

Occupy This

One lie is that there is
strength in numbers.
I submit this lone wolf.
I keep the moon at bay, aloof.
No one to encumber,
yet you tremble at the sound

of me. I see your friends abound,
coffee'd and tea'd, the spirit
of your cafe'd crowd
and book clubs that read aloud.
Not one of you has a lick of merit
in the street among broken lamps,

or wet and hungry in the protest camps.
When I hold up my cardboard sign
you look away. It has grown dark
outside, but this sleeping in the park
and marching in a raging line
sure keeps me from being alone.

LAURA L. SNYDER

Degrees of Hunger

My skin is white, my college degree within
a calfskin folder on a shelf behind poverty
and bright smiling pictures. I was the wide-eyed one
with promise, they said. And when I married,
I thought love and cornflakes would be enough—
in America. After all, no parent on my block
had to teach that a husband might find it
inconvenient to work. How would I know
the way to thrift stores, government
surplus food, or the way to lift lowered eyes?

My car knows all the stops now,
even ones to grocery produce managers.
I ask for cuttings from lettuce,
overripe fruit, dried up vegetables—
anything
they could set out...*for my chickens.*

Now my children are grown. They
do not remember homemade bread and pasta,
nor our diet of unending soup. They
do not remember me on the lawn sorting
boxes of moldy fruits, paring away
with a sharp knife, living
on what I pieced from myself.
They remember hand-me-down clothes,
forms for free lunch programs, their mom
firm-lipped about their dad,
and her voice saying, "No, I'm sorry
we can't—there's no money."

THE POET SPIEL

righteous rock

the efficacy of the rock
   superior to the bomb
   so readily expired
the rock shot back
   upon its sender
   at a fraction of the cost
then shot again
   and shot right back
   to be shot again and again
one rock
   in simple continuity
the choice of weapons
   for us
   uncivilized of men
and shot and shot
   but barely worn
though bloodied
   here or there
weighted with such effective
   hatred of the bearer
and isn't it a picnic
   to be had by all
that rock

until
at last
it chooses
   what it knows best
just and lasting
embeds itself
   deep in the gall
   of the one
   who shot it first

naked arms

they may be hungry
but they are not cold

they learned first
not to be cold
not to wear a coat
because there was no coat

you see them at grunt work
on highways on rooftops on farms you see
them pushing snow pushing manure
no coat   like they are not cold
tho you are freezing everyone is freezing

the old ones survived
the border crossing
determined to tolerate
anything for a penny
just for this opportunity
they could not afford to be cold

their kids' kids' kids still crawl out
from beneath old truck beds
or plywood lean-tos down at the tracks
to walk to school to learn english
with their faces scrubbed
but without coats   with naked arms

you want to say:
are you hungry
are you cold
tho you know they are not cold

if you gave them your coat
they would not wear it

they do not wear coats

bulk beans or rice suffice

but they are not cold

SCOTT T. STARBUCK

Chinese Dream on the Canadian Border

I have two books: the Bible
and Kesey's *Sometimes a Great Notion,*
and the guard says
"只有一本图"
translation: "Only one book!"

The language of the Bible
is trees, mountains, rivers,
and can never be destroyed
so, Lord forgive me,
I choose Kesey's book.

Its torso river cover
looks like the Siletz in Oregon
where I trolled for sea-run cutts
between the Movie House
below Coyote Rock
and my deckhand Tristan's house
on Siletz Bay.

Maybe I choose the book because
Merry Prankster Kesey
was a Coyote too, of sorts,
symbolic, trickster, appearing
as an omen, vanishing in thickets
like his character Hank Stamper who said
"And if Oregon was to get into it
with California I'd fight for Oregon."

Now California, Oregon, and
Washington all speak Chinese,
and I wonder aloud
"How long before Mt. Rushmore
has the face of "黄帝?"

translation: "Yellow Emperor?"
"Already does," says the guard in English.

In Kesey's book there is a disoriented deer
swimming out to sea
like throngs of migrants to Canada,
two languages of man,
visceral and wise,
Heart of the Pacific Northwest
that changes all invaders,
gift and sacrifice and renewal beyond
anyone's wildest dreams.

In Photoshop®

If I stretch a dollar far enough
George Washington looks like George Bush
and the eyed-pyramid is a haunted house.
Serial numbers blur into cloud wisps.

Outside, there is rain on the window,
a tall mountain with men
who look like ants
in a Chinese landscape triptych.

As one of those ants,
I grew up believing in fireplaces,
astronauts, and the Pledge of Allegiance
in Catholic school.

When I look back at Photoshop®,
and try to restore the dollar
to its original proportions,
I have a hard time seeing

it's still a dollar.

CAROL STEINHAGEN

Hats

In grainy films JFK is forever young,
irresistible,
all that Irish hair blowing free.
Exposed.
As if he had no secrets.
Our mothers got weak-kneed.
Dads packed away their hats.

In photos of Depression bread lines
all the men wear hats.
Their fedoras are carefully creased.
Their newsboy caps smartly raked.
It's as if their sweatbands had trapped
the shame, the refusal to stand out there
before the camera's cold stare.
Day after day they came, inching
toward some inchoate promise,
eyes shaded by the brims of their hats.

Now we know JFK's secrets.
No one has secrets anymore.
The hair falling rakishly
over men's foreheads refuses custom,
promises improvised nights.
So many possibilities.
So little restraint.
So much hair blowing in the wind.

SUSAN K. STEWART

Poem for a New Economy

I realize finally I have no marketable skills.
Corporations, as it happens, leave orphaned words
on doorsteps
along with those who know how to shelter them
and sometimes rise to their defense.

There is, for instance, no opening for a *good* cook,
just good,
—but having mastered gluten
free sugar
free heart
healthy low
fat no fat
and how to wave
the yellow, orange, and white flag of the ten year old.

As to manual labor, I am a hard worker
but slow.
At speed, I make mistakes
at everything but sex
—the only profession in which the amateur
looks down on the careerist.

An interviewer might learn I am good in a crisis.
My resume might list my instinct
for knowing the locations of emergency rooms,
a fluency with the languages of paramedics, counselors, and funeral directors.
That days later I am fragile as old memories
and tear-prone
I keep (professionally) to myself.

And with these meager qualifications,
Where among the files of
Human Resources
will they house my application?

JULIE STUCKEY

From Out These Eyes

those footsteps could be mine...I taste dust
and feel that crunch, that gravel
beneath thin soles.
Some say *thank God* or *but for the grace*—
but I know it is not He who tramples
on the backs of those without. It is I.
I have been one who turned away, who could not
name the suffering, even as my turning
let the suffering continue. Now my children,
waiting to stumble into their light,
carry this cowardice, my indeterminate shadow.

I have released tree branches from unseasonable
snow and ice—heard their rustle of thanks
even as some limbs cracked from the weight.
And the marching columns continue
into the night and on into tomorrow, swelling
and dwindling according to the whims of those same
gods who lined us up and made us recite
litanies of shoulds and oughts with no thought
for others. *We take care of our own. Don't
tread on me.* I am mute with the shame of silence.
It is where I come from, that choked-off inability to speak.
Groping for a way, there is a depth I long to touch.
It is here, behind the watching, that I wait.

WALLY SWIST

Outside the Box

I would notice her walking down the hill after work
on my way to the parking lot, usually near the entrance

to the physical plant. I was always impressed with her
courage as she strolled with a more diminutive natural

woman and two men who would walk apart from them
but with them at the same time. After the various

post-ops, I observed her gangly duckling princess
maleness diminish and transform itself into a feminine

version of who she was to be. Undisputedly,
the stroll with the diminutive natural woman became

that of belonging to the sisterhood and its mystery
and less like the two men who still walked with them

and not with them. If you had not been privy to observe
her transformation in passing, then you couldn't easily

discern that she had the change executed and met
the challenge of becoming transgender. Her courage

is what offered me most resilience, that steadfastness
in the face of what the world might have thought about

her choosing. I would need to summon my own courage
when I was unfairly terminated and would no longer walk

down the hill to the parking lot due to bullyism on the job
that was all too similar to the Nazi *Beer Hall Putsch*—

the malicious smile of the new Store Director
and the *machismo* and *machisma* of his henchmen,

the bottomless stupidity in their eyes in their buddying-up
to exercise the fascism of the corporation,

the philosophy of there being no thoughts outside the box.
That reminded me of when I was ganged up on

and beaten in the sandbox, as a child,
by some of the other boys who flexed their naked bravado,

how after I was pummeled with fists
I would try to stand up and spit out the dirt in my mouth.

The City of Nails

Here it is, up ahead, beyond
   that hairpin turn where
      old values are blacklisted,

where law abides by its own
   private pool of sewage
      curiously like poor Narcissus,

where death is the street punk
   telling us this is the arrival,
      the departure no one has ever

prepared for enough,
   where inverted road signs
      map the new archetype

and billboards advertise
   wash-and-wear sex,
      the most refreshing colas,

totems of refined taste, where
   the marriage of anima and animus
      is just another one-night stand

for *machisma* and *machismo.*
   Here it is. Go ahead.
      Welcome to the city of nails

where every telephone pole
   lining the farthest limits
      to the main strip is condemned

for crucifixion. Bear down.
   Head on the dark side
      unravels like black crepe.

JUDITH TERZI

Exile

> *Mexican exiles in El Paso can see their pasts across the river*
> —Los Angeles Times, *12/31/10*

An assassin's bullet killed my Celedonio last year.
He was an angel in the school Nativity play.
Confusion fills our converted garage in El Paso.
There's safety here, but who are our neighbors?
In Juárez I didn't work with hands but words.
We crossed the Río Bravo & wait for asylum papers.

There I was a writer for the Juárez newspaper.
I make tacos and burritos in my kitchen this year.
Darkness follows us though we never speak the word.
Our 3-year-old Jesús doesn't go outside to play.
We stick to ourselves, don't talk to the *vecinos*
in this barrio of taquerías & garages in El Paso.

They say we don't have to lock our doors in El Paso.
But we follow the scoreboard in *El Diario*,
hear about the killing of a cousin or a neighbor:
over 3,000 *Juareños* murdered last year.
We wonder what games Calderón is playing.
Obras son amores, y no buenas palabras.

His actions should be tougher than his words.
As the sun dips, we stare at the horizon beyond El Paso.
The 320-foot flagpole comes into view; we imagine plays
on the soccer field where I reported for the paper.
Celedonio's in the photo from his baseball game last year—
precioso in a Sapitos uniform standing next to our *vecino,*

his coach. *Mi'jito* hit a home run; the whole neighborhood
cheered. The coach died in a bloodbath. No other word.
I miss my mesquite tree, the garden I started last year.
Here, there is alley & concrete in the barrio of El Paso.

I read articles about us in American newspapers;
they say we are tormented by the exile, the replay

of *la violencia*. If only I could see Los Indios play
or celebrate a baptism in our once intact *vecinidad*.
But there are only funerals announced in the paper.
Asylum means we can't return home. We send *palabras*
to family, maybe chocolates; we're stuck in El Paso
like the bridge over the Río. Jesús is quiet for his 3 years.

Celedonio plays...we hear laughter, only Spanish words
beyond El Paso & the Río. We're 10 minutes from our *vecinos*.
10 minutes for a paperless life. Celedonio lived for 7 years.

MARK THALMAN

Celilo Falls

The frothing river cascades
over basalt cliffs, pounding
giant drums, thundering for miles.
Salmon launch themselves
out of white water—
fall back into the roaring torrent.

For ten thousand years,
men have come here
to spear Chinook
or stand on scale-slick,
mist-covered platforms
with long-handled dip nets.

When the flood gates closed,
the river began to rise,
and the spectacular rumbling
which had filled the air
for millions of years slowly died.
Families lining the rim
were consumed by silence.

While the water inched higher,
planks and poles from scaffolds
drifted away like their lives.
The next to drown were petroglyphs,
village sites, and burial grounds,
under a deep lake
to generate cheap electricity.

In the legend, five Swallow Sisters
built a barrier preventing the salmon
from returning. Coyote tricked them,
destroyed their dam, and the flood
washed away the land leaving Celilo Falls.
May Coyote bring back the falls again.

CHARLES THIELMAN

Watering coleus after midnight, during wartime

I rise from the loam of a dream
and watch heavy winds and rain whip streams
      over roof-tops and asphalt
    as night-shift cars flick on by,
      their headlights lit opals.

Blue spruce stands above the river
close to that train's wail and pull of boxcars,
boxcars empty or packed wood floor to steel ceiling,
    clanking on to a bridge over the river
      as I water coleus after midnight.

Tony Bennett croons his heart out from my stereo
into my workroom's votive- and lamp-lit, incense-filled, air.

I snip a few leaves to guide this coleus higher and higher,
then water the neighboring dracaena,

thinking of the word *lluvia,* español for rain,
of *borrasca,* gale-force winds, *lluvia y borrasca,*
of my friends and their children sleeping and dreaming
  as it rains and rains buckets this March night.

      Praying for all,
seeing how these plants spread their branches, fronds and leaves,

    praying for all the young soldiers to stop killing one another,
      firing, firing into a blinding sandstorm in the desert

    as generals finger arrows over maps

    commanding the ghosts they create.

All the People

Rush hour throttles dawn silent, bird
songs filed below glyphs of exhaust.
Jackhammers cube the air, our city
remaking its image, rebranding, suits
in line at the bus-stop as a circle of children
makes churches, steeples, with their hands,
people being fingers fed by one artery.

Boxed headlines cite evidence
the willfully stupid gather their given power.
Volleys strobe from the vortex
of the dimmed as they ratchet up
their shit-flinger, see the white-eyed souls
backstroke over shallows in a city full of sharks.

Frequencies warped into subliminal
umbilical iPod-pumping classic rock,
on the bus watching for the brunette artist,
her easel and canvas often perched near
bridge and river as she translates winds
funneled through bridge legs into colors.

I'd be wondering which brush would best
spade a layer of yellow to the east of indigo
and silhouette the unrelenting mothers long-faced
into years of searching morgues and trenches
for their children lost to war and abduction.

My work hours spent marketing trends
reset monthly under a sky of Muzak.
Seeing how greed divides our chorus
into competing sound bites, I often
visit the tall, dark Lincoln statue
across from the art museum after work.
Yesterday, the painting of a child grasping
chain-link upslope from a gray river hit hard.

After so many years, many people continue
to work on saving our environment, being
unable to slink into a recliner at the end
of another whatever day and let the media
fashion wants into soul-sized magnets
as humanity bows walking backwards
into preparing for yet another war.

ALICE TOPOROFF WALLACE

Bus Stop

Tiny slivers
sharp as razors
sting

It's the end of the day in the city.
I'm at my usual corner waiting with fellow commuters;
we mouth disconnected small talk, trying not to inhale
blue air. Red light changes, people cross, passing siren screams.

Dreadlocked Deborah, fast-talking Sales Rep, something
to do with computers, mutters and looks at her watch;
laid-back Luis, Customer Service, he of the endless
eyelashes, bites his customary evening apple; I shiver
and button my coat. The bus is late.

Next to me, a tall, angular woman, Calvin Klein glasses,
shifts her briefcase, wipes her red drippy nose,
sniffs an opinion about the annual CityFest Jamboree
she "certainly won't be attending because they, you know
what I'm saying, *baptistsblacksgayshispanicsmuslimsjews,*
seem to be taking over everywhere." The moment splinters.

Tiny slivers
Sharp as razors

Words. Just words.
A few gut-tightening words
tossed with casual malice
into our waiting-to-go-home world.
No one speaks. No one moves.
The bus arrives.
Some bleed. Some don't.

CONNIE WALLE

'57 Chevy

He torques, wipes
oils, polishes
washes and dries.

He circles her
three times
touches her lovingly.

Carefully backs
her down
the driveway.

The letter comes.
A country he has never heard of before
needs his undivided
attention.

It's been a long time,
but without tears
Mama sold
    the Chevy today.

ED WERSTEIN

The Way Philanthropy Works

At concerts in Rockefeller Center
sensitive ears can still hear the cries and wails
of the Ludlow miners
and their wives and children
slaughtered on the picket line in Colorado, 1914.

Without opening a book,
keen eyes can read
the lost lives of unschooled steel workers
on the facades of thousands of libraries,
part of the Carnegie bequest.

And who remembers
the abandoned artistic ambitions
of the aluminum smelters, the oil riggers,
and the bank tellers who labored
so the Mellon family could endow
the National Gallery of Art?

DAN WILCOX

Pindar's Shrimp

Eating the last of the Gulf shrimp
poets stuttering about oil, about water
I think of another, more ancient, poet
who said, "Water is the best of things."

But where would Pindar place oil
not what he knew squeezed from olives
but the compost of dinosaurs, their plants
that we burn so wantonly?

Water is the best of things, but oil
oil is the darkest, spreading darkness
even as it burns for light.

What Really Happened

was that it was nurses, doctors, civil
engineers & soldiers in clown suits
who invaded Afghanistan in October, 2001.

The children laughed, thought that
Americans were really funny & liked them.

Their parents found work building roads
& schools & water treatment plants.

They even got TVs & small refrigerators &
the electricity stayed on all day & night too.

What really happened was that when
the dusty men from caves with Kalashnikovs
told them Americans were evil & wanted
to kill them everyone laughed & no one
wanted to be a suicide bomber.

CHRISTOPHER WOODS

Make Room! Make Room!

Their field is wide
Enough for the soldiers
From every country in time.

Crowded, always crowded,
Not an inch to turn
Away from so much grief.
But still the god calls to them,
"Make room! Make room!"

And so they bunch closer
Together, a Roman soldier,
A Viet Cong boy in black,
Doughboys without faces,
Grudgingly make room
For the new war dead
Arriving unexpectedly
At all dark, bloody hours.

Death's badges identify them
Victims of catapults, boiling oil,
I.E.D.s, napalm and gas,
Sticks and stones,
All the tools of the wars
That lead them all here
Where there is no need
To speak, only to acknowledge
Tears and every once-proud flag.

MARIANNE WORTHINGTON

Working Girl Blues

In memory of Hazel Dickens, 1935-2011

When she went to look for factory work
and needed a place to live,
she searched the vacancies among the row
houses built for those who toiled
as beer-bottlers, bakers, meat-packers, maids.

On Baltimore streets the boarding house signs
warned *No Dogs or Hillbillies.*
She settled in Little Appalachia
amid the rough refugees—
her people—who journeyed north when the mines

mechanized and the coal bosses ordered
the mountains stripped and gutted.
She had found a way in, unearthed her voice,
the one she had used back home
when her Daddy would call her out to sing

for neighbors. But now there was a bad taste
in her mouth, a misery
in her singing as if all the world's wrongs
had come to live in her throat.
She chased that bile with words that cut open

a truth like the coal seams her brothers had
bared in the mines. *If you can't
stand by me, don't stand in my way,* she wailed.
Her tunes hypnotized sickness
and beat back grief and lack. She bellowed down

mean men and they stopped making fun of the
lonesomeness in her accent.
A rebel girl intoned for us and we
listened. We're listening still, but
it's hard to tell the singer from the song.

ANDRENA ZAWINSKI

Bittersweets for Camellia

*Segregation of white and colored children
in public schools has a detrimental effect...*
—Chief Justice Earl Warren, Brown v Board of Education

The classroom air choked with chalk dust
and floor wax, but huddled in close outside
on the fire escape landing at West Park School,
in McKees Rocks, we tasted chocolates plucked
from inside the heart-shaped Russell Stover box
where my mother hid her bonbons—
a bite for you, a bite for me. The Baby Ruths
from the corner candy store cost you
your milk money, Camellia, the outside melt
the color of your hands, the nougats and creams
inside light as my fingertips breaking into the chew.

We hummed our sticky sweet delights stowed inside
our Butterick jumper pockets, until the teacher
flagged me across the stretch of cement school yard
over to the iron gate that led back to your row house
and my tenement, across hopscotch lines chalked in—
a clumsy journey, swings clanging against
a school bell ringing in the end of play for the day.

Don't do that, the teacher whispered
like a secret, like a sin, words that traveled
from a playground of a schoolhouse long razed
in Pittsburgh all the way to Charleston
one springtime where in the Old Slave Market
I plucked from a ballast of stone a camellia,
a scentless bloom that fell apart in my hands,
flew in a flurry of spent petals into the wind.

Don't do that, words that confounded children
in the Sunflower State finally able to walk

to school, or those giggling under cherry blossoms
facing the sprawl of Capitol monuments, or others
digging toes in sand on the Chesapeake Bay
sharing a peach—*a bite for you, a bite for me.*

Or evenings, their chins perched on hands,
listening together in the quiet, to nightingales
flowering the dogwood—but this bothers me now:
Camellia, the last time I was in Pittsburgh
so many years after, I saw you boarding
the 14C back to West Park, arms brimming
with McCrory store bundles, a little
light-skinned girl latched to your waist,
and I stood there frozen to the curb, unable
to wave my hand, unable to raise my voice,
dumbstruck by words drifting in from a teacher
whose face or name I cannot recall:
Don't do that, she said, its bittersweet
still on my tongue.

The Pickers

Stronger and stronger, the sunlight glues
The afternoon to its objects...
—*from* Against the American Grain, *Charles Wright*

The pickers, backbent and dozens abreast, rise before the sun
    past the blonde grasses, behind the concertina wire
running between Soledad and Salinas, move in squats,
    toss artichokes from sun-pocked fields into pickup cabs,
    calloused fingers pricked by the thorny thistles.

They pour seeds into rivulets of dry earth
    that will burst into lettuce, chard, the great bouquets
    of broccoli and cabbage along El Camino Real's humpback hills
where foremen watch, arms folded across their dusty boredom
    and the long light of days stretching inside another summer.

Bodies at work, long after limbs tire, long after chests heave
    beneath bird-bone beads, abalone shells, scapulars dangling
    from red strings, or even chains of gold glinting off the sun,
    faces muffled in scarves and hoods, sweat scenting the air,
backbent and dozens abreast, birthing a history of earth.

And so they move, the pickers, silhouetted against the horizon,
    westerly winds crossing groves and vineyards farther north,
    farther south, they move, follow the crops, follow the seasons,
Steinbeck's ghost among the harvest gypsies in the fields,
    pen in one hand, pail in the other, working towards some end.

As sure as low clouds cool the day down, the bodies turn
    toward evening, lay down the ache of the field in the stretch of legs,
    slope of shoulders, move toward dreams of the unburned, pain-free,
    unafraid, unspent paper in the pocket for some half-hold on a home
    on the road, birds skittering tree branches at sunset,
    pecking at the unpicked.

CONTRIBUTORS

Work by **Austin Alexis** has appeared in *Barrow Street, The Journal, The Pedestal Magazine, The Writer,* in the anthologies *Off the Cuffs* (Soft Skull Press), *Empty Shoes: Poems on the Hungry and the Homeless* (Popcorn Press) and in other publications. He received an Editor's Choice Award from *Mobius: The Poetry Magazine,* an Artist Grant from the Vermont Studio Center and a Bread Loaf Writers' Conference Scholarship.

Gilbert Allen has lived in Travelers Rest, SC, since 1977. He is the Bennette E. Geer Professor of Literature at Furman University. His fourth collection of poems, *Driving to Distraction* (Orchises, 2003), was featured on *The Writer's Almanac* and *Verse Daily.* In 2007 his sequence of poems "The Assistant" received the Robert Penn Warren Prize from *The Southern Review.*

Jennifer Arin is the author of the poetry book *Ways We Hold* (2012). Her verse and essays have been published in both the U.S. and Europe, in *The AWP Writer's Chronicle, The San Francisco Chronicle Sunday Book Review, Gastronomica, Puerto del Sol, Poet Lore, ZYZZYVA, Paris/Atlantic Review,* and *The Chronicle of Higher Education,* among many others. Her awards include a grant from the NEH, a PEN Writer's Fund grant, a Poets & Writers Writers-On-Site Residency, and funding from the Spanish Ministry of Culture. She teaches in the English Department at San Francisco State University.

Kate Bernadette Benedict is the author of the poetry collections *Here from Away* (2003) and *In Company* (2011). She lives in Riverdale, New York where she edits the online poetry journals *Umbrella* and *Tilt-a-Whirl.*

Nina Bennett is the author of *Forgotten Tears: A Grandmother's Journey Through Grief.* In 2006, she was selected to attend the Delaware Division of the Arts Masters' Workshop in poetry. Nina's poetry has appeared in journals and anthologies, including *Avatar Review, Burning Word, Drash, Northwest Mosaic, Pulse, Alehouse, Panache, Yale Journal for Humanities in Medicine, The Smoking Poet, Oranges & Sardines, Philadelphia Stories, The Broadkill Review, Slow Trains Literary Journal, Spaces Between Us: Poetry, Prose and Art on HIV/AIDS* and *Mourning Sickness.* Nina is a contributing author to the Open to Hope Foundation.

Kevin Brown is Professor at Lee University and an MFA student at Murray State University. His poems have appeared or are forthcoming in *The New York Quarterly, REAL: Regarding Arts and Letters, Folio, Connecticut Review, South Carolina Review, Stickman Review, Atlanta Review,* and *Palimpsest,* among other journals. He has also published essays in *The Chronicle of Higher Education, Academe, InsideHigherEd.com, The Teaching Professor,* and *Eclectica.* He has a book of poetry, *Exit Lines* (Plain View Press, 2009); a chapbook, *Abecedarium* (Finishing Line Press, 2011); and the forthcoming book, *They Love to Tell the Stories: Five Contemporary Novelists Take on the Gospels.*

Melissa Carl's work has appeared or is forthcoming in a variety of print and online publications, including *Amoskeag: The Journal of Southern New Hampshire University, cellpoems, CircleShow, Freshwater, In Posse Review, Melusine, Off the Coast Magazine, The Broken Plate Review, The Fledgling Rag, Third Wednesday,* and a number of anthologies. Her second full-length poetry volume, *Brutal Allure,* was published in 2011. She is a regular, featured reader at various venues in the Central Pennsylvania and Maryland regions and has appeared on a public television program devoted to poetry. She resides in York, PA, and Oak Island, NC, with her husband and son.

David Chorlton has lived in Phoenix, AZ, since 1978 when he moved from Vienna, Austria, with his wife. Born in Austria, he grew up in Manchester, close to rain and the northern English industrial zone. In his early twenties he went to live in Vienna and from there enjoyed many trips around Europe. In Arizona, he has grown ever more fascinated by the desert and its wildlife, the theme of his 2008 collection from FutureCycle Press, *The Porous Desert*. In 2008, he won the Ronald Wardall Award from Rain Mountain Press for his chapbook *The Lost River*, and in 2009 the Slipstream Chapbook Competition for *From the Age of Miracles*. Most recently, *The Taste of Fog*, the result of a long-standing interest in Vienna's shadow side, appeared as his first work of fiction. He currently serves as Poetry Coeditor for FutureCycle Press.

Alex Cigale's poems have appeared in *Colorado Review, Green Mountains Review, North American Review, Tampa Review,* and *The Literary Review* plus online in *Asymptote, Drunken Boat,* and *McSweeney's.* His translations from the Russian appear in *Ancora Imparo, Cimarron Review, Literary Imagination, Modern Poetry in Translation, PEN America,* and *Two Lines.* He is an Assistant Professor at the American University of Central Asia in Bishkek, Kyrgyzstan.

James Cihlar is the author of *Undoing* (Little Pear Press, 2008) and *Metaphysical Bailout* (Pudding House Press, 2010). *Rancho Nostalgia* is forthcoming in 2013 from Dream Horse Press. His writing appears in *American Poetry Review, Prairie Schooner, Lambda Literary Review, Court Green, The Awl, Mary, Rhino,* and *Forklift, Ohio.*

Jim Clark is the Elizabeth H. Jordan Professor of Southern Literature and Chair of the Department of English and Modern Languages at Barton College in Wilson, North Carolina. He was born in Byrdstown, Tennessee, and educated at Vanderbilt University, the University of North Carolina at Greensboro, and the University of Denver. His books include *Notions: A Jim Clark Miscellany, Dancing on Canaan's Ruins, Handiwork,* and *Fable in the Blood: The Selected Poems of Byron Herbert Reece.* He has also released a CD of original poems and Appalachian folk music, *Buried Land,* and two CDs, *Wilson* and *Words to Burn,* with his folk-rock band *The Near Myths.* His second solo CD, *The Service of Song,* released in 2010, features his musical settings of twelve poems by the north Georgia "farmer-poet" Byron Herbert Reece.

Kelly Clayton was born and raised in Louisiana. Writing poetry full time, she has earned a living as a cook, waiter, companion for the elderly, publisher's assistant, and housekeeper. She currently lives in Brooklyn with her husband and youngest of four sons and teaches creative writing in the New York City public schools.

Nominated for the *2009 Best of the Net Anthology* and the *2009 Best New Poets* (University of Virginia), **Chella Courington** teaches literature and writing at Santa Barbara City College. Her recent work appears or is forthcoming in *The Los Angeles Review, lo-ball, Gargoyle Magazine, Opium Magazine, Pirene's Fountain,* and *Everyday Genius.* "Diana loved anything orange" was runner-up in *The Collagist* 2009 flash fiction contest. She's published three chapbooks: *Southern Girl Gone Wrong, Girls & Women,* and *Paper Covers Rock.*

Barbara Crooker's books are *Radiance,* winner of the 2005 Word Press First Book Award and finalist for the 2006 Paterson Poetry Prize; *Line Dance* (Word Press, 2008), winner of the 2009 Paterson Award for Excellence in Literature; and *More* (C&R Press, 2010). Her poems appear in a variety of literary journals and many anthologies, including *Good Poems for Hard Times, Good Poems for American Life* (Garrison Keillor, editor of both) (Viking Penguin) and the *Bedford Introduction to Literature.*

J. P. Dancing Bear is the author of 10 collections of poetry, most recently *The Abandoned Eye* (FutureCycle Press, 2012). Other books include *Inner Cities of Gulls* (2010, Salmon Poetry), *Family of Marsupial Centaurs* (Iris Press, 2011), and *Fish Singing Foxes* (Salmon Poetry, 2012). His poems have been published in *Mississippi Review, Third Coast, DIAGRAM, Verse Daily* and many other publications. He is editor for the *American Poetry Journal* and Dream Horse Press. Bear also hosts the weekly hour-long poetry show, *Out of Our Minds,* on public station, KKUP and available as podcasts.

Erica Dawson's collection of poems, *Big-Eyed Afraid* (The Waywiser Press, 2007) won the 2006 Anthony Hecht Prize. Her poems have appeared in *Best American Poetry 2008, Barrow Street, Birmingham Poetry Review, Blackbird, Harvard Review, Literary Imagination, Poetry: A Pocket Anthology* (7th edition), and other anthologies and journals. Erica is an assistant professor of English and Writing at University of Tampa, where she serves as poetry editor for *Tampa Review* and teaches in the university's MFA program.

Diane Elayne Dees's social and political poems have been published in many journals and anthologies. Diane published the social/political blog, *The Dees Diversion,* and also blogged for *Mother Jones.* She currently publishes *Women Who Serve,* a blog about women's professional tennis.

Anthony DiMatteo's poems have cropped up in current or recent issues of *Avatar Review, Denver Syntax, Right Hand Pointing, Smartish Pace, Tar River Poetry,* and *Wilderness House Literary Review.* Essays and reviews have been spotted in *Connotations, Notes and Queries,* and *Spenser Studies.* He remains bullishly committed to teaching the relations of literature, art and writing at the New York Institute of Technology. He enjoys living on Long Island with his wife, son, two dogs and canary. Feel free to leave a trace at his tentsite: anthonydimatteo.wordpress.com.

David Ebenbach's poetry has been published in the *Beloit Poetry Journal, Subtropics,* and the *Hayden's Ferry Review,* among others. He is also the author of two collections of fiction: *Between Camelots* (University of Pittsburgh Press, winner of the Drue Heinz Literature Prize and the Great Lakes Colleges Association's New Writer Award), and *Into the Wilderness* (forthcoming from Washington Writers' Publishing House, winner of the WWPH Fiction Prize). His non-fiction exploration of the creative process, *The Artist's Torah,* is forthcoming from Cascade Books. He recently received fellowships to the MacDowell Colony, the Virginia Center for Creative Arts, and the Vermont Studio Center, and an Individual Excellence Award from the Ohio Arts Council.

Alan Elyshevitz is a poet and short story writer from East Norriton, PA, with poems appearing most recently in *Snail Mail Review, Sliver of Stone,* and *Tidal Basin Review.* In addition, he has published two poetry chapbooks: *The Splinter in Passion's Paw* (New Spirit) and *Theory of Everything* (Pudding House). Currently he teaches writing at the Community College of Philadelphia.

Margot Farrington is the author of two collections, most recently *Flares and Fathoms* (Bright Hill Press). She has been awarded poetry residencies at the I-Park Foundation in East Haddam, CT, Platte Clove in upstate NY, and The Clock Tower in NYC, in 2010 and 2011, respectively. Farrington's poetry appears in anthologies in the U.S. and the U.K. Performance works include such venues as EMPAC at RPI, Miller Theater at Columbia University in NYC, West Kortright Centre, Optosonic Tea Series in NYC, and others. Interviews and readings may be accessed via the archives of Art On Air International Radio and WGXC.

Rupert Fike's collection, *Lotus Buffet,* was published by Brick Road Poetry Press in 2011. Two of its poems have been nominated for a Pushcart Prize, and he was recently named Finalist (poetry) as Georgia Author of the Year 2011. His work has appeared in *Rosebud, The Georgetown Review, A&U America's AIDS Magazine, Natural Bridge, The Atlanta Review, The Cortland Review, storySouth, The Blue Fifth Review* and others. His non-fiction book, *Voices from The Farm,* accounts of life on a spiritual community in the 1970s, is now in its second printing. One of his poems is inscribed in a downtown Atlanta plaza.

Alissa Fleck is a poet from Minneapolis, currently residing in New York City, where she is pursuing her MFA at The New School. Her work has appeared previously in Argos Books anthology *Why I Am Not a Painter, The Grinnell Review,* and elsewhere.

Barbara Gabriel is a poet, writer and salvage artist who has been gathering writing material for fifty years while impersonating a chef, cruise director, ice cream scooper, sailor, child advocate, landscaper, package designer, dive master, log cabin builder, and a really bad waitress. Barbara grew up in Minnesota along Highway 61 and has traveled and lived in North and South America, Turkey, North Africa, Europe, Southeast Asia and the Caribbean. She has been published in the online journal of topical poetry, *Poetry24.* Barbara currently calls Portland, Oregon home, alongside her husband Brian and dogs Gracie and Scout.

Bill Glose is a former paratrooper, a Gulf War veteran, and author of the poetry collection, *The Human Touch* (San Francisco Bay Press, 2007). In 2011, he was named the Daily Press Poet Laureate. His poems have appeared or are forthcoming in such journals and magazines as *Narrative Magazine, New York Quarterly,* and *Chiron Review.*

Les Gottesman's first published poems were in Ted Berrigan's *C magazine* in 1965. More recently, his poems have appeared in *Juked, Beatitude, Harper's, Antioch Review,* and *Columbia Review.* Les has been a teacher in San Francisco for over 30 years. He received his MFA in Writing from California College of the Arts in 2011.

Michael Gregory is the author of several poetry books and chapbooks including *The Valley Floor, Hunger Weather 1959-1975,* and *re Play.* "Pins and Needles" is included in *Mr America Drives His Car* (Education in Reverse Press, 2011). Before retirement, he was for many years an internationally recognized toxics activist, authored numerous articles, papers and monographs on environmental politics, and was an active participant in development of such citizen right-to-know programs as the North American Pollutant Release and Transfer Register and the Stockholm Convention on Persistent Organic Pollutants. Since 1971, he has lived off-grid in the high desert grassland of southeast Arizona ten miles from the US-Mexico border where he raises organic fruits and vegetables.

Lois Marie Harrod's eleventh book, *Brief Term,* poems about teaching, was published by Black Buzzard Press (2011); her chapbook *Cosmogony* won the 2010 Hazel Lipa Chapbook Contest (Iowa State University); her chapbook *Furniture* won the 2008 Grayson Press Poetry Prize. She won her third poetry fellowship from the New Jersey Council on the Arts in 2003. Over 400 of her poems have been published online and in print journals including *American Poetry Review, Blueline, The MacGuffin, Salt, The Literary Review, Verse Daily* and *Zone 3.* A Geraldine R. Dodge poet, she teaches Creative Writing at The College of New Jersey. Read her work on loismarieharrod.com.

Michelle Hartman has published recently in *Poetry Quarterly, The Pedestal Magazine, Elegant Rage/The Woody Guthrie Anthology, Raleigh Review, San Pedro River Review, Pacific Review, Concho River Review, RiverSedge, Illya's Honey* and various anthologies: *Overseas in The SHOp* (Ireland), *Blue Print Review* (Germany), *Five Poetry Journal* (Australia), and *The Applicant* (Nepal). She was a juried poet in the 2009 Houston Poetry Festival. She is editor of the online journal, *Red River Review,* and holds a BS in Political Science-Pre Law from Texas Wesleyan University and a Certificate in Paralegal Post Grad studies.

Born in Atlanta, poet **M. Ayodele Heath** is a graduate of the MFA program at New England College. His debut poetry collection, *Otherness,* is available from Brick Road Poetry Press. Honors include a 2009 Dorothy Rosenberg Prize and a McEver Visiting Chair in Writing at Georgia Tech. He was awarded fellowships from Cave Canem, Summer Poetry at Idyllwild and the Caversham Centre for Writers & Artists in South Africa. He received a grant in Literary Arts from the Atlanta Bureau for Cultural Affairs.

Kathleen Hellen is a poet and the author of *The Girl Who Loved Mothra* (Finishing Line Press, 2010); *Umberto's Night*—winner of the 2012 Washington Writers' Publishing House Prize in poetry—is forthcoming. Her poems have appeared in *American Letters & Commentary; Barrow Street; Cimarron Review; The MacGuffin; Natural Bridge; Nimrod; Prairie Schooner; Swink; Sycamore Review;* among others; and her work was featured on WYPR's *The Signal.* Other awards include the Washington Square Review, James Still and Thomas Merton poetry prizes. She is senior editor for the *Baltimore Review.*

T. L. Hensel has been published in *Pickup Poets Anthology of Short Stories* and *Poetry, Encore, Oh, Georgia, Creative Collaboration in the Southeast, Reach of Song, Shout Them from the Mountain Tops,* and *English, Too* (a Russian textbook). He began writing at 40 years of age. He is owner of a mechanical contracting firm, has been married to Joan over 35 years, and their two sons serve in the United States Army.

Graham Hillard is founding editor of *The Cumberland River Review* and an associate professor of English at Trevecca Nazarene University, in Nashville, TN. His work has recently appeared in *32 Poems, Apalachee Review,* and *Controlled Burn* and is forthcoming in *The Journal, New Millennium Writings,* and *Regarding Arts and Letters.*

H. Edgar Hix grew up in the American South. Hix has spent most of his adulthood in the North, in Minneapolis, MN. Hix has held a variety of jobs: warehouseman, library clerk, legal secretary, call center representative, and system analyst. Hix has been publishing poetry, and other types of writing, for some 40 years. Hix lives with his wife, seven cats and one dog, who suffers the cats with (usually) quiet dignity. Recent publications have been in *Right Hand Pointing, Waterways: Poetry In the Mainstream, Priscilla Papers, bear creek haiku, Mutuality,* and *Time of Singing.*

Karen Paul Holmes, a freelance writer, splits her time between Atlanta and the Blue Ridge Mountains. Poetry credits include *Poetry East, Atlanta Review, Wild Goose Poetry Review, Dead Mule School for Southern Literature* and *The Sow's Ear Poetry Review.* In July 2012, she taught a writing class at John C. Campbell Folk School in Brasstown, NC.

Paul Hostovsky is the author of four books of poems, most recently *Hurt Into Beauty* (FutureCycle Press, 2012). Other books include *Bending the Notes, Dear Truth,* and *A Little in Love a Lot.* His poems have won a Pushcart Prize and been featured on *Poetry Daily, Verse Daily, The Writer's Almanac,* and *Best of the Net* 2008 and 2009. To read more of his poetry, visit his website at paulhostovsky.com.

Joseph Hutchison is the author of 13 collections of poems, including *Thread of the Real, The Rain at Midnight, Bed of Coals* (winner of the 1994 Colorado Poetry Award), *House of Mirrors,* and *The Undersides of Leaves.* Born and raised in Denver, Colorado, Hutchison teaches graduate level writing courses at the University of Denver's University College but makes the bulk of his living as a writer. He lives with his wife Melody Madonna in Indian Hills, a small community in the foothills southwest of Denver.

Jason Irwin grew up in Dunkirk, NY, and now lives in Pittsburgh, PA. He holds an MFA from Sarah Lawrence College. His first volume of poetry, *Watering the Dead* (Pavement Saw Press), won the 2006/2007 Transcontinental Poetry Award. His *Some Days It's A Love Story* won the 2005 Slipstream Press Chapbook Prize. His one-act play "CIVILIZA-TION" had its staged reading debut on April 24, 2010, at The Living Theatre, NYC. "Undone," a one-man/one-act play was performed at the Willits Shakespeare Theatre September 29–October 2, 2011 as part of *Scripted: an Evening of Original One Act Plays.*

Roshanda Johnson began to write songs for her singing group, The Dreamers when she was only six years old. As she grew, her song writing blossomed into poetry. She graduated from Debakey High School in 1997 and soon after entered Houston's Poetry Scene, quickly becoming a force to be reckoned with. In 2002 she graduated with highest honors from U of H with a Bachelor's in Interdisciplinary Studies. After teaching for one year, she quit her job, stepped out on faith, and began to tour the country performing spoken word. She performed with "Two Black Ladies in Chairs," "Liquid Soul," the Latin band "Rey of Light," as well as opening for various rap, r&b, and soul artists. In addition to spoken word, she has performed in and produced several plays, including *AIR Imagination* at the Ensemble Theatre and *The Inside* at Silver House Theatre. She currently plays the role of Stephanie in *Gospella The Divine Inheritance.* She resides in Houston, TX with her dog Chompers.

Lawrence Kessenich won the 2010 Strokestown International Poetry Prize. His poetry has been published in *Atlanta Review, Poetry Ireland Review, Cream City Review, Istanbul Review, Ibbetson Street,* and many other magazines. His chapbook *Strange News* was published by Pudding House Publications in 2008. Another chapbook was a semi-finalist for the St. Lawrence Book Award and finalist for the Spire Press Chapbook Contest. In 2011, his full-length collection, *Before Whose Glory,* was a semi-finalist for the Off the Grid contest and his poem "Underground Jesus" was nominated for a Pushcart Prize. Kessenich has also published essays, one of which was featured on NPR's *This I Believe* and appears in the anthology *This I Believe: On Love.* His plays have been produced in Massachusetts and Colorado.

Alan King is a poet and journalist living in the DC metropolitan area. His poems have appeared in *Alehouse, Audience, Boxcar Poetry Review, Indiana Review, MiPoesias* and *RATTLE,* among others. He's also the senior program director for DC Creative Writing Workshop, a Cave Canem fellow, VONA Alum, and MFA candidate at the University of Southern Maine's Stonecoast program. He has been nominated for both a Best of the Net selection and a Pushcart Prize. His first collection of poems, *Drift,* will be published in 2012 by Willow Books.

Robert S. King lives in the Blue Ridge Mountains of Georga. His poems have appeared in hundreds of magazines, including *California Quarterly, Chariton Review, Hollins Critic, Kenyon Review, Lullwater Review, Main Street Rag, Midwest Quarterly, Negative Capability, Southern Poetry Review, Spoon River Poetry Review,* and *Writers' Forum.* He has published three chapbooks (*When Stars Fall Down as Snow,* Garland Press 1976; *Dream of the Electric Eel,* Wolfsong Publications 1982; and *The Traveller's Tale,* Whistle Press 1998) and two full-length collections (*The Hunted River* and *The Gravedigger's Roots,* Shared Roads Press 2009). In late 2011, he stepped down as Director of FutureCycle Press to spend more time writing. He continues to serve the press as Poetry Coeditor.

John Laue has edited *Transfer* and been Associate Editor of *San Francisco Review.* He presently coordinates the monthly reading series of The Monterey Bay Poetry Consortium. His fourth book, *A Confluence of Voices,* has just come out from Finishing Line Press. In addition to writing, his main interest is mental health. He has served as member and Co-Chair of the Santa Cruz County Mental Health Advisory Board.

Sean Lause teaches courses in Shakespeare, The American Short Story and Composition at Rhodes State College in Lima, OH. His poems have appeared in *The Minnesota Review, Another Chicago Magazine, Poetry International, The Alaska Quarterly, The Beloit Poetry Journal, European Judaism, The Saranac Review* and *Upstart Crow.*

Brenda Kay Ledford is a member of North Carolina Writers' Network, North Carolina Poetry Society, Georgia Poetry Society, and Byron Herbert Reece Society. Her work has appeared in *Our State, The Reach of Song, Appalachian Heritage, Pembroke Magazine,* and other journals. She received the Paul Green Award for her poetry chapbooks, *Patchwork Memories, Shew Bird Mountain,* and *Sacred Fire.* Recently, Brenda coauthored *Simplicity* with her mother, Blanche L. Ledford. The book is a collection of prose and poetry about Clay County, North Carolina.

Laura LeHew is an award-winning poet with over 375 poems appearing in over 175 national and international journals and anthologies such as *Ambush Review, Collecting Life Poetry Anthology, Eleven Eleven, Filling Station, PANK, Uncanny Valley* and others. *It's Always Night, It Always Rains* is forthcoming in 2012 from the Medulla Review. *Beauty* (Tiger's Eye Press) is in its third printing. Laura received her MFA in writing from the California College of the Arts, writing residencies from Soapstone and the Montana Artists Refuge, interned for *CALYX Journal,* and edits *Uttered Chaos* (utteredchaos.org). She has seven cats, one husband, and never sleeps.

Jean Thurston Liebert, age 93, is a former teacher now living in mid-Willamette Valley, Oregon. She writes poetry, short stories and has written a novella, *Another World.* Her published work is included in *Apricot Memories,* a non-fiction history of the apricot industry in California; Linn Benton Community College's Collections; the Oregon Writers Colony anthology, *Take a Bite of Literature;* and the progressive online site *New Verse News.* In addition to receiving recognition for her SHE Project poetry, Jean's 2010 fiction was cited as notable by the Oregon Writers Colony.

Deborah Mashibini teaches as an adjunct Instructor at Southern Illinois University Edwardsville, St. Louis Community College, and Ranken Technical College. Her poems have appeared in *Drum Voices Revue, Untamed Ink, Kaleidoscope Magazine, Riverbluff Review, Sestina: Six Women Poets,* and *The Harwood Anthology.* In conjunction with her work with non-profit organizations, she helped to edit and publish *Where we can read the wind* and *Blindness Isn't Black,* two anthologies of work by Missouri writers and artists with disabilities; *The Best of the Enabled Writer, Prose and Poetry by New Mexican's with Disabilities,* and *Forgotten Voices Unforgettable Dreams,* a collection of work by homeless writers and artists in NYC.

Andrew Shattuck McBride has poems published or forthcoming in *Platte Valley Review, Haibun Today, Generations of Poetry, bottle rockets, Dreams Wander On: Contemporary Poems of Death Awareness, Mu: An International Haiku Journal, Prune Juice: A Journal of Senryu and Kyoka, A Hundred Gourds, Shamrock Haiku Journal, The Bellingham Herald,* and *Clover, A Literary Rag.* His poem "Desire (Padden Creek Winter)" was runner-up in the 2011 *Clover, A Literary Rag* contest; his poem "Boulevard Park" won a merit award in the 2009 Sue C. Boynton Poetry Contest. He has also edited four poetry collections.

Jim McGarrah's poems and essays appear frequently in many literary journals and magazines. He is the author of two award-winning books of poetry, *Running the Voodoo Down* (Elixir Press, 2003) and *When the Stars Go Dark* (Main Street Rag, 2009); two memoirs, *A Temporary Sort of Peace* (Indiana Historical Society Press, 2007), which received the 2010 Eric Hoffer Award for Legacy Nonfiction and was a finalist for the Montaigne Medal, and his newest book of nonfiction, *The End of an Era* (Ink Brush Press, 2011). He has also published a novel, *Going Postal,* and written a play, *Split Second Timing,* that received a Kennedy Center ACTF award in 2001. He is editor, along with Tom Watson, of the anthology *Home Again: Essays and Memoirs from Indiana* (Indiana Historical Society Press, 2007). Any of his books may be ordered from the links on this web site: web.me.com/jimmcgarrah. He lives in Louisville, KY.

Nancy Carol Moody's work has appeared in *The MacGuffin, The New York Quarterly, Bellevue Literary Review, The Carolina Quarterly,* and *Salamander.* She is the author of *Photograph With Girls* (Traprock, 2009) and has just completed a new manuscript titled *Negative Space.* She can be found online at nancycarolmoody.com and lives in Eugene, OR.

Janell Moon is poet laureate of the bay-side city of Emeryville, CA, just across the bay bridge from San Francisco. She has published eleven books of spiritual non-fiction and poetry. Last year she won the RAW ArT Press Experimental Poetry/Prose Prize for a hybrid, "Salt and Paper." She won the 2007 Main Street Rag Editor's Prize for a manuscript and the 2005 Stonewall Prize among others.

George H. Northrup is President (2006–) of the Fresh Meadows Poets in Queens, NY, a Board member of the Society that selects the Nassau County Poet Laureate, and former President of the New York State Psychological Association.

Scott Owens is the author of 10 collections of poetry and over 800 poems published in journals and anthologies. He is editor of *Wild Goose Poetry Review,* Vice President of the Poetry Council of North Carolina, and recipient of awards from the Pushcart Prize Anthology, the Academy of American Poets, the NC Writers' Network, the NC Poetry Society, and the Poetry Society of SC. He holds an MFA from UNC Greensboro and currently teaches at Catawba Valley Community College. He grew up on farms and in mill villages around Greenwood, SC.

Judith Pacht's book of collected poems, *Summer Hunger,* was published in October, 2010, and her chapbooks, *User's Guide* and *St. Louis Suite* were published in 2009 and 2010. Pacht's manuscript *Vectors* was a finalist for the 2008 Philip Levine Prize, and her poem, "Waterville, Maine" won Honorable Mention in the 2007 Robert Frost Award and the 2007 Robinson Jeffers Tor House Prize for Poetry competitions. She was first place winner in the Georgia Poetry Society, Edgar Bowers competition. A three-time Pushcart nominee, Judith Pacht's work includes poems published in

Ploughshares, Runes, Phoebe, Cider Press Review and *Foreign Literature* (Moscow, Russia). Her poems have also appeared in numerous anthologies. Her chapbook, also her first poetry collection, *Falcon* (Conflux Press), was published in 2004.

A native Detroiter, **Christina Pacosz**' poetry/writing has appeared in books, literary magazines and online journals for half a century. *Notes from the Red Zone*, originally published by Seal Press (1983), was the inaugural winner of the ReBound Series (Seven Kitchens Press, 2009). *How to Measure the Darkness* will launch the Seven Kitchens Summer 2012 Limited Edition Chapbook Series on the Summer Solstice. She lives in Kansas City, Missouri with her husband and their former street cat.

Lee Passarella is a founding member and senior literary editor of *Atlanta Review* and acted as editor-in-chief of *FutureCycle Poetry* and Coreopsis Books. His poetry has appeared in *Chelsea, Cream City Review, Louisville Review, The Sun, Antietam Review, Journal of the American Medical Association, The Formalist, Cortland Review,* and many other periodicals; recent publications include *Concho River Review, Stickman Review,* and *Rock & Sling. Swallowed up in Victory*, Passarella's long narrative poem based on the American Civil War, was published by White Mane Books in 2002. In addition, he has published two other books of poetry: *The Geometry of Loneliness* (David Roberts Books) and *Sight-Reading Schumann* (Pudding House Publications).

Garth Pavell most recently published in *Glass, Carcinogenic Poetry, Canary, Poetry Super Highway* and *The Writing Disorder.* Garth lives in Brooklyn, NY, and earns his living writing for a nonprofit organization.

Joel Peckham is the author of three collections of poetry: *Movers and Shakers, The Heat of What Comes,* and *Nightwalking.* Recently Academy Chicago Publishers released his literary memoir, *Resisting Elegy: Essay on Grief and Recovery.* Individual poems and essays have appeared in many journals, including *The Black Warrior Review, The North American Review, Prairie Schooner, River Teeth,* and *The Southern Review.* He lives with his wife, Rachael, and son, Darius, in Huntington, WV.

Diana Pinckney lives and teaches in Charlotte, NC. Published in *RHINO, Atlanta Review, Cream City Review, Cave Wall, Green Mountains Review, FutureCycle Poetry, Tar River Poetry, MacGuffin, Calyx* and many other journals and anthologies, she has four collections of poetry: *Fishing with Tall Women* (contest winner in North and South Carolina), *White Linen, Alchemy,* and *Green Daughters,* released in 2011. She is the winner of the 2010 EKPHRASIS Prize. Pinckney has recently been awarded the Atlanta Review's 2012 International Poetry Prize. She has been nominated for a Pushcart Prize more than five times. Her website is dianapinckney.com.

Kenneth Pobo's latest publications include three chapbooks for 2011. *Closer Walks* was published by Thunderclap Press. Deadly Chaps published a chapbook of his "tweet fiction" called *Tiny Torn Maps,* and Green Fuse Press published a chapbook entitled *Contralto Crows.*

David Radavich's recent poetry collections are *America Bound: An Epic for Our Time* (2007), *Canonicals: Love's Hours* (2009), and *Middle-East Mezze* (2011), which focuses on Iraq, Palestine, and Egypt. His plays have been produced across the U.S., including six Off-Off-Broadway, and in Europe. He was recently given The MidAmerica Award for his life-time contributions to Midwestern literature and scholarship.

M. S. Rooney and her husband, poet Dan Noreen, live in Sonoma, CA. Her work has been published in journals including *The Cortland Review, The Laurel Review, Other Voices,* and *3 AM Magazine.*

Linwood Rumney's poetry has appeared or is forthcoming in *Potomac Review, Carolina Quarterly, Poetry Quarterly, Quercus Review, Superstition Review,* and *Cold Mountain Review,* among others. He is a 2010 recipient of a fellowship from the Writers' Room of Boston and an emerging artist grant from the St. Botolph Club Foundation. He currently resides in Cincinnati.

Tina Schumann's manuscript *As If* (Parlor City Press) was awarded the Stephen Dunn Poetry Prize for 2010. Her work was named a finalist in the 2011 National Poetry Series. She is the recipient of the 2009 American Poet Prize from *The American Poetry Journal.* Her poems received honorable mention in *The Atlantic Monthly* 2008 Poetry Writing Contest as well as the 2010 *Crab Creek Review* contest. In 2011, her work was nominated for a Pushcart. She holds an MFA from Pacific Lutheran University, and her work has appeared in various publications including *The American Poetry Journal, Ascent, Cimarron Review, Crab Creek Review, Harpur Palate, PALABRA, PARABOLA, Poemeleon* and *Poetry International.*

Eric Paul Shaffer is author of five books of poetry, including *Lāhaina Noon* and *Portable Planet.* His poetry appears in *North American Review, Slate, Ploughshares,* and *The Sun Magazine;* Australia's *Going Down Swinging, Island* and *Quadrant;* Canada's *CV2, Dalhousie Review, Event,* and *Fiddlehead;* Éire's *Poetry Ireland Review* and *Southword Journal;* England's *Stand* and *Magma;* and New Zealand's *Poetry NZ* and *Takahe.* Shaffer received the 2002 Elliot Cades Award for Literature, a 2006 Ka Palapala Po'okela Book Award for *Lāhaina Noon,* and the 2009 James M. Vaughan Award for Poetry. His novel, *Burn & Learn,* was published in 2009. He teaches at Honolulu Community College.

Marian Kaplun Shapiro is the author of a professional book, *Second Childhood* (Norton, 1988), a poetry book, *Players In The Dream, Dreamers In The Play* (Plain View Press, 2007) and two chapbooks: *Your Third Wish* (Finishing Line, 2007); and *The End of the World, Announced On Wednesday* (Pudding House, 2007). As a Quaker and a psychologist, her poetry often addresses the embedded topics of peace and violence, often by addressing one within the context of the other. A resident of Lexington, she was named Senior Poet Laureate of Massachusetts in 2006, in 2008, and in 2010.

San Francisco-based poet **Michael Shorb**'s work reflects an abiding interest in environmental issues, history, and the lyrical form. His poems have appeared in over 100 magazines and anthologies, including *The Nation, The Sun, Michigan Quarterly Review, Queen's Quarterly, Poetry Salzburg Review, Commonweal, Rattle, Urthona, Underground Voices, The Great American Poetry Show* and *European Judaism.* His collection, *Whale Walkers Morning,* will appear in Winter 2013 from Shabda Press. We were saddened to learn of his death shortly before the publication of this anthology.

Nancy Simpson is the author of three poetry collections: *Across Water, Night Student* and most recently *Living Above the Frost Line, New and Selected Poems* published 2010 by Carolina Wren Press. She also edited the anthology *Echoes Across the Blue Ridge* (2010). She holds an MFA from Warren Wilson College. Simpson's poems have been published in *The Georgia Review, Southern Poetry Review, Seneca Review, New Virginia Review, Prairie Schooner* and in other literary magazines.

Ron Singer (ronsinger.net) writes libretti (*Rimshot, Deeds, Carla the Copy-Shop Girl*); poetry (e.g., *alba, Arlington Literary Journal, Borderlands, The Texas Poetry Review, The Brooklyn Rail, Contemporary Rhyme, elimae, Evergreen Review, The Hampden-Sydney Poetry Review, New Works Review, Poetry Midwest, Waterways: Poetry in the Mainstream, The Windsor Review,* and *Word Riot*); essays and reviews about African subjects (e.g., *Evergreen Review, The Georgia Review, opendemocracy, Poets & Writers online,* and *The Wall Street Journal*); and prose fiction and satire (e.g., *The Avatar Review, big bridge, The Brooklyn Rail, Defenestration, diagram, Drunken Boat, elimae, Ellipses, ghoti, Mad Hatters' Review, Oregon Literary Review, Paper Street, SN Review, Third Wednesday, Willow Review,* and *Word Riot*). He recently made three protracted visits to Africa, where he interviewed pro-democracy activists for a new book, *Uhuru Revisited* (Africa World Press/Red Sea Press, forthcoming).

J. D. Smith's third collection of poems is *Labor Day at Venice Beach* (published in August 2012). In 2007 he was awarded a Fellowship in Poetry from the National Endowment for the Arts.

M. R. Smith is a poet residing and writing in Boise, Idaho. His work has or will appear in publications such as *Punchnel's, The Red River Review, Poetry Breakfast, The Camel Saloon,* and *Your Hands Your Mouth.*

Laura L. Snyder uses a slanted profile to scratch out words in hard-back journals from rainy Seattle. Find her latest in *Windfall, Labletter, The New Verse News,* and in the recent anthologies: *Poets of the American West, Classified: Prose Poems,* and *Cradle Songs.* Laura was nominated for a Pushcart and for Dzanc's "Best of the Web 2010." Her chapbook, *Winged,* came out this spring from Flutter Press.

The Poet Spiel is frequently published online and in independent press journals in Nepal, Wales, Britain, Indonesia, Scotland, Ireland, Canada and the U.S. with diverse works of personal conflict, social commentary and satire noir. His most recent book is *barely breathing,* an anthology of poetry spanning his ten years as a writer, published by March Street Press. Learn more about his body of short stories, poetry, spoken word and his lifelong career as a visual artist at thepoetspiel.name.

Scott T. Starbuck, whose 31-minute activist/nature poem interview is posted on the Internet (classroom.sdmesa.edu/sstarbuck2/ScottStarbuck2011Radio.mp3), works as a Creative Writing Coordinator and World Literature Coordinator at San Diego Mesa College. Recent poems appear in *occupypoetry.org, Scythe, cur*ren*cy, Niche Magazine, Blue Lotus Review,* and *Untitled Country Review.* New work is forthcoming in *Cream City Review* and *Two Thirds North* at Stockholm University in Sweden.

Carol Steinhagen is a recovering English professor, having retired from Marietta College to undertake the life of a poet and gardener. She hopes that she is a better poet than gardener. Her recently published work appears in *Earth's Daughters, The Aurorean, Collecting Life: Poets on Objects Known and Imagined,* and *Caesura.*

Susan K. Stewart lives, works, and writes in Lexington, Kentucky.

Julie Stuckey grew up in Pennsylvania, graduated from the University of Delaware in business and currently lives in Pawling, New York. Her poems have appeared online and in print in *Apropos Literary Journal, Ardent, Blast Furnace, Prairie Wolf Press Review, Seven Hills Review, Shark Reef,* and *Verdad,* among others, and in anthologies from Little Red Tree Publishing and From Under the Bridges of America. She has received Finalist or Honorable Mention in several contests.

Wally Swist's book, *Huang Po and the Dimensions of Love*, was selected by Yusef Komunyakaa as a co-winner in the Crab Orchard Series Open Poetry Competition, and was published by Southern Illinois University Press in August 2012. His previous book, *Luminous Dream*, was selected as a finalist for the 2010 FutureCycle Poetry Book Prize. *The Friendship of Two New England Poets: Robert Frost and Robert Francis*, a scholarly monograph, was published by The Edwin Mellen Press in 2009. An audiobook of 65 of his poems, *Open Meadow: Odes to Nature*, was released by Berkshire Media Arts in April 2012. A new book, *Winding Paths Worn through Grass*, will be published by Visual Artists Collective, of Chicago, in early 2013.

Judith Terzi's poetry has received awards and recognition from *dotdotdash, Gold Line Press, Mad Hatters', Newport Review, River Styx*, and elsewhere. Most recent work has appeared or is forthcoming in *Blast Furnace, CHEST, Poemeleon, Qarrtsiluni, Raintown Review* and *Spillway*. For many years a high school French teacher, she also taught English at California State University, Los Angeles, and in Algiers, Algeria. *Sharing Tabouli* was published by Finishing Line Press in 2011.

Mark Thalman is the author of *Catching the Limit* published by Fairweather Books (2009). His poems have appeared in *Carolina Quarterly, CutBank, Pedestal Magazine*, and *Verse Daily*, among others. He received his MFA from the University of Oregon, and he teaches English in the public schools. Thalman is the editor of poetry.us.com. He lives in Forest Grove, Oregon. For more information, please visit markthalman.com.

Charles Thielman was raised in Charleston, SC, and Chicago, educated at red-bricked universities and on city streets. He has worked as a youth counselor, truck driver, city bus driver and enthused bookstore clerk. Recently married on a Kauai beach, a loving grandfather for five free spirits, his inspired work as poet, artiste and shareholder in an independent Bookstore's collective continues. He organizes readings at the store and serves on the Board of his county writers' organization, which is currently promoting the Poetry Box Project—the boxes are like curbside realtor's boxes, but with copies of poems inside for unsuspecting passerby. His chapbook, *Into the Owl-Dreamed Night*, is available from Uttered Chaos Press (utteredchaos.org).

Alice Toporoff Wallace grew up in Brooklyn, NY, married a North Carolinian and spent the first two years of married life in South Carolina raising turkeys. Although the farm venture didn't work out, she did learn how to milk a cow. Writing poetry came later. Her poems have appeared in *Kakalak—An Anthology of Carolina Poets, Main Street Rag, Iodine Poetry Journal, Bay Leaves* and *Pinesong Awards*, published by the North Carolina Poetry Society. She lives in Charlotte, NC, with her husband of sixty years— and not a turkey in sight.

Connie Walle resides in Tacoma, WA. She is President of Puget Sound Poetry Connection, which she founded 20 years ago. She received the 2003 Faith Beamer Cooke. Also the 1998 Margaret K. Williams. She hosts the "Distinguished Writer Series and Open Mic" readings monthly, with a grant from the City of Tacoma Art Commission. She founded and coordinated for eight years Our Own Words, a county-wide teen writing contest, now in its 16th year. She is currently part of the anthology *Pontoon* (Floating Bridge Press). She is a mother of three, grandmother of seven, and currently retired.

Ed Werstein spent 22 years in manufacturing and union activity. He now works as an employment counselor helping job seekers. His sympathies lie with the poor and working people of the world. He advocates for peace and against corporate power. His poetry has appeared in *Verse Wisconsin, Blue Collar Review, New Verse News, Mobius Magazine,* and several other publications.

Dan Wilcox is host of the Third Thursday Poetry Night at the Social Justice Center in Albany, NY, and is a member of the poetry performance group "3 Guys from Albany." As a photographer, he claims to have the world's largest collection of photos of unknown poets. His poems have been published in *Out of the Catskills, Post Traumatic Press 2007, Chronogram, Poetica* and in numerous small press journals and anthologies, on the internet, as broadsides, and in self-published chapbooks. His chapbook *boundless abodes of Albany* is available from Benevolent Bird Press of Delmar, NY. You can read his blog at dwlcx.blogspot.com.

Christopher Woods is the author of a prose collection, *Under a Riverbed Sky.* His play, *Moonbirds,* about census-takers at work in an unpopulated desert country, was produced in New York City by Personal Space Theatrics. He lives in Houston and in Chappell Hill, Texas.

Marianne Worthington is co-founder and poetry editor of the online literary journal *Still: The Journal* and poetry editor for *Now & Then: The Appalachian Magazine.* She is editor of the *Motif* anthology series from Motes Books and the 2010 recipient of the James Baker Hall Memorial Prize in Poetry sponsored by *New Southerner* magazine. Her poetry chapbook is *Larger Bodies Than Mine* (Finishing Line Press, 2006). She lives in Williamsburg, KY.

Andrena Zawinski's poetry collection, *Something About* from Blue Light Press in San Francisco, is a PEN Oakland Josephine Miles Award recipient. Her first collection, *Traveling in Reflected Light* (Pig Iron Press), won a Kenneth Patchen Prize in Poetry. She runs the Bay Area Women's Poetry Salon for which she is editor of their *Turning a Train of Thought Upside Down: An Anthology of Women's Poetry.* Zawinski is also the Features Editor for PoetryMagazine.com and a teacher of writing.

ACKNOWLEDGMENTS

Grateful acknowledgment is made to the following publications in which many of these poems first appeared:

"After Long Days Visiting the Nursing Home, I Return to the Office" by Kate Bernadette Benedict, *Gin Bender* and in the author's book *In Company.*

"After the War, the War" by Robert S. King, *The Foundling Review.*

"American Intrinsic" by Nancy Carol Moody, *PANK.*

"American Materialism: the Rococo Period" by George H. Northrup, *Performance Poets Association Literary Review.*

"and falling, fly" by Michelle Hartman, *The Raleigh Review.*

"Annual Pigeon Shoot, Higgens, PA" by Marian Kaplun Shapiro, *Out Of Line* and in the author's book, *Players In The Dream, Dreamers In The Play.*

"Bees in Lavender" by Gilbert Allen, *The Georgia Review.*

"Belly Song" by Kathleen Hellen, *Yellow Medicine Review.*

"Bittersweets for Camillia" by Andrena Zawinski, *Psychological Perspectives: A Semi-annual Journal of Jungian Thought.*

"Bread" by Lois Marie Harrod, *Earth's Daughters.*

"Brink" by Alan King, *Brink.*

"Bus Stop" by Alice Toporoff Wallace, *Bay Leaves.*

"Catalog" by Barbara Crooker, *Poetz.*

"Cheap Mangos" by David Chorlton, *Slipstream.*

"Coming Summer" by David Chorlton, *Minotaur.*

"A Congress of Monsters" by Kathleen Hellen, *The Potomac: A Journal of Poetry and Politics.*

"Conjugal Rites" by Scott Owens, *Main Street Rag.*

"Country Data" by J. D. Smith, *Helix.*

"Degrees of Hunger" by Laura L. Snyder, *Red River Review.*

"The Dreamlife of Dr. Bledsoe's Inner Pickanniny" by M. Ayodele Heath, *Crab Orchard Review.* Also appears in author's book, *Otherness* (Brick Road Poetry Press).

"Economics" by David Chorlton, *Main Street Rag.* Also appears in the author's book, *A Normal Day Amazes* (Kings Estate Press).

"Election Season" by J. P. Dancing Bear appears in the author's book, *Conflicted Light.*

"Exile" by Judith Terzi, *BorderSenses.*

"Falcon" by Judith Pacht, Phoebe and in author's book *Summer Hunger.*

"'57 Chevy" by Connie Walle, *Raven Chronicle.*

"Four Gates to the City: South" by Christina Pacosz is a section from a longer poem originally appearing in the author's book, *Some Winded, Wild Beast.*

"Friday Afternoon in Brooklyn" by David Ebenbach, *Sow's Ear Poetry Review.*

"Habeas Corpus (Show Me the Body)" by Alex Cigale, *The Potomac: A Journal of Poetry and Politics.*

"Huntingdon, Tennessee: Age 20" by Graham Hillard, *The Los Angeles Review.*

"Ideology Begins at Home" by James Cihlar, *Smartish Pace.*

"Insomnia" by Chella Courington, *wicked alice.*

"Lament for Louisiana" by Diane Elayne Dees, *The Raintown Review.*

"The Laramie Project" by Nina Bennett, *Panache.*

"Listen Hard Enough" by Ron Singer, *New Works Review.*

"Make Room! Make Room!" by Christopher Woods, *New Verse News.*

"Memorial" by M. S. Rooney, *Americas Review*.

"Minor Prophet" by Graham Hillard, *Hiram Poetry Review*.

"Murder by the (Wrong) Numbers" by Christina Pacosz, *New Verse News*.

"naked arms" by The Poet Spiel, *St. Vitus Press*.

"On the Amish" by J. D. Smith, *Dark Mountain*.

"One Late Night" by Jim Clark, *Notions: A Jim Clark Miscellany*.

"The Pickers" by Andrena Zawinski, *The Progressive Magazine* and *Tule Review*.

"Pins and Needles" by Michael Gregory, *New American Dream*.

"A Poem that's Not a Song or Set in the South" by Erica Dawson, *Harvard Review*.

"Progress" by Brenda Kay Ledford, *Western North Carolina Woman*.

"Reality TV" by Michelle Hartman, *descant*.

"The Red House in Washington" by Eric Paul Shaffer, *The 365 Project*.

"righteous rock" by The Poet Spiel, *AlphaBeat*.

"Roy's Five-and-Dime" by Nancy Carol Moody, *The South Dakota Review*.

"Shrapnel" by Kate Bernadette Benedict, *The Raintown Review*.

"Some Days It's a Love Story" and "Cadillacs" by Jason Irwin, *Living Forge Journal*.

"Some Lullabies" by Linwood Rumney, *Cold Mountain Review*.

"The Stinky Lady" by Kate Bernadette Benedict, appeared in the author's book, *Here From Away*.

"To the Man on Death Row, Waiting" by David Chorlton, *Chiron Review*.

"24 Cents" by Deborah Mashibini, *Untamed Ink*.

"The Very Last Supper" by Gilbert Allen, *South Carolina Review*.

"'Want to Know Who We Are?'" by Melissa Carl, *CircleShow*.

"The Way Philanthropy Works" by Ed Werstein, *New Verse News* and *Mobius: The Journal of Social Change*.

"Watering coleus after midnight, during wartime" by Charles Thielman, *Dona Nobis Pacem / Grant Us Strength* (anthology).

"What Really Happened" by Dan Wilcox, *Poeming the Prompt* (author's chapbook).

"Blocking the ▮▮▮▮▮▮▮▮ Banner" by Laura LeHew is a redaction of the actual poem written by Francis Scott Key in 1814, "Defense of Fort McHenry." The poem was later put to the tune of (John Stafford Smith's song) "The Anacreontic Song," modified somewhat, and retitled "The Star Spangled Banner." Congress proclaimed "The Star Spangled Banner" the U.S. National Anthem in 1931.

Cover art by Nimalan Tharmalingam; cover and interior book design by Diane Kistner (dkistner@futurecycle.org); Gentium Book Basic text with Arial titling

ABOUT FUTURECYCLE PRESS

FutureCycle Press is dedicated to publishing lasting English-language poetry and flash fiction books, chapbooks, and anthologies in both print-on-demand and ebook formats. Founded in 2007 by long-time independent editor/publishers and partners Diane Kistner and Robert S. King, the press incorporated as a nonprofit in 2012. A number of our editors are distinguished poets and authors in their own right, and we have been actively involved in the small press movement going back to the early seventies.

Our annual anthology, *FutureCycle*, combines poetry and flash fiction. The FutureCycle Poetry Book Prize and honorarium is awarded annually for the best full-length volume of poetry we publish in a calendar year. We are dedicated to giving all authors we publish the care their work deserves, making our catalog of titles the most distinguished it can be, and paying forward any earnings to fund more great books.

We've learned a few things about independent publishing over the years. We've also evolved a unique, resilient publishing model that allows us to focus mainly on vetting and preserving for posterity the most books of exceptional quality without becoming overwhelmed with bookkeeping and mailing, fundraising activities, or taxing editorial and production "bubbles." Come see us at www.futurecycle.org.

THE FUTURECYCLE POETRY BOOK PRIZE

All full-length volumes of poetry published by FutureCycle Press are considered for the FutureCycle Poetry Book Prize and honorarium. The book ranked the best by the judges for a given calendar year will be announced as the prize-winner in the subsequent year. The winning poet will receive an honorarium of 20% of our total net royalties from all poetry books and chapbooks the press sells online in the year of the book's publication. The winner will also receive copies of, and be accorded the honor of guest-judging, books for the prize in the subsequent year. Please refer to the general guidelines on our website before submitting your work to us.

www.ingramcontent.com/pod-product-compliance
Lightning Source LLC
Chambersburg PA
CBHW060048100426
42742CB00014B/2738